Freedom Farmers

Freedom Farmers

*Agricultural Resistance and the
Black Freedom Movement*

MONICA M. WHITE

The University of North Carolina Press CHAPEL HILL

Library of Congress Cataloging-in-Publication Data
Names: White, Monica M. (Monica Marie), 1967– author.
Title: Freedom farmers : agricultural resistance and the black
   freedom movement / Monica M. White.
Other titles: Justice, power, and politics.
Description: Chapel Hill : University of North Carolina Press, [2018] |
   Series: Justice, power, and politics | Includes bibliographical
   references and index.
Identifiers: LCCN 2018017919| ISBN 9781469643694 (cloth : alk. paper) |
   ISBN 9781469663890 (pbk. : alk. paper) | ISBN 9781469643700 (ebook)
Subjects: LCSH: African Americans—Agriculture—History. | African
   Americans—Social conditions—History. | African Americans—
   Political Activity—History. | Agriculture, Cooperative—United
   States—History. | Food sovereignty—United States. | Food
   supply—Political aspects—United States—History. | Freedom
   Farms Corporation (Sunflower County, Miss.) | North Bolivar
   County Farm Cooperative (Mound Bayou, Miss.) | Federation of
   Southern Cooperatives. | Detroit Black Community Food Security
   Network. | Black lives matter movement.
Classification: LCC E185.86 .W38756 2018 | DDC 305.896/073—dc23
   LC record available at https://lccn.loc.gov/2018017919

Cover photo: DBCFSN's Food Warriors program at the Shrine
of the Black Madonna in Detroit, July 2017. © Jeremy Brockman,
http://www.BrockmanDP.com.

A previous version of chapter 2 was published in a different form as
"'A Pig and a Garden': Fannie Lou Hamer and the Freedom Farms
Cooperative," *Food and Foodways: Explorations in the History and
Culture of Human Nourishment* 25, no. 1 (2017): 20-39.

Contents

Illustrations

Acknowledgments

There are many to thank for their support as I researched and wrote *Freedom Farmers*. I appreciate this opportunity to express my gratitude to those who have made this research process enriching, rewarding, and life changing. Not unlike the unending ball of yarn, each question in this research led me to a person who was willing to not only answer but who also asked further questions and connected me to others who were able to help me engage the topic of black farmers and agricultural resistance at a deeper level. There are many projects upon which this one can be built, and this is only a first installment in unearthing the hidden narratives of black farmers who create and participate in agricultural cooperatives as a strategy of resilience and resistance.

When I found myself stuck in the research process, there were so many friends and colleagues who were willing to organize book club meetings, campus brown bag presentations, or community meetings where I was able to present my framework and talk through my findings. There were always those who extended themselves to me, who offered words of encouragement, or who connected me to someone new. For all those individuals not named here but who offered endless advice and support in the writing process, I am grateful.

To the members of the Detroit Black Community Food Security Network, you have become my family. Your work, vision, and drive helped me identify the questions that would give my life purpose and meaning. To Baba Malik, Mama Aba, Mama Ebony, Baba Kwamenah, Mama Linda, Mama Nefer Ra, and all of the members of the DBCFSN, I am eternally grateful for the love, direction, patience, and endless support you have given to me and for all your efforts to transform a city, build a food movement, and to create a just and sustainable world. You taught me that home is a verb. There were many others in the Detroit food justice movement who have supported me, offered me chances to share my ideas, and pushed and loved me through all of it. Thanks especially to Ashley Atkinson of Keep Growing Detroit for early reads and for your support of this work and Patrick Crouch of Earthworks Urban Farm.

Other food justice activists have embraced this project and offered support and feedback: Mama Asantewaa Harris, who introduced me to Freedom Farm many years ago; Blain Snipstal, Black Dirt Farm; Dara Cooper, National Black Food Justice Task Force; LaDonna Redmond, Campaign for Food Justice Now; Tracy McCurty, the Black Belt Justice Center; Eric Holt-Giménez, Institute for Food and Development Policy; Drs. Ife and Tdka Kilimanjaro, University of KMT Press; Baba Rashid Nuri, Truly Living Well; Dr. Owusu Bandele, Southeast African American Farmers Organic Network; and the brilliant organizer and now ancestor Mama Cynthia Hayes. I'm so encouraged by all of you who do this work and your willingness to embrace these ideas as part of a framework for liberation. You all have supported my research ideas, offered me feedback, and showed me a reflection of myself and my work that made it easy to keep going.

A huge thank-you goes to my former colleagues at Wayne State University: David Fasenfest, Heidi Gottfried, and Sarah Swider, who have always believed in my work. Special thanks to David Goldberg for his early support and for directing me to additional research sources I would otherwise have missed. Thanks also to Kerry Ann Rockquemore of the National Center for Faculty Development and Diversity who, in the "ideal day" exercise, helped me realize the trajectory that would transform my career by convincing me that there was room for my ideas in the academy. To my friends in the African American Studies Department at the University of Illinois at Urbana-Champaign, you offered an early space to try out the logic of my approach, jump-starting my intellectual inquiry into agricultural resistance. Lou Turner offered countless hours of reading and answering my calls, and along with his partner Ruby Mendenhall, organized and hosted a writing group session in their home with friends and colleagues from UIUC; Helen Neville, Imani Bazzell, Michael Flug (retired archivist from the Vivian Harsh Collection at the Carter G. Woodson

Regional Library in Chicago), and Safiya and Otis Noble of the University of Southern California embraced the book idea and gave me hours of transcribed notes from feedback that helped shape the direction of the book. Also in attendance was Sundiata Cha-Jua, who gave me the title *Freedom Farmers* and has remained a constant source of support for this project from its early inception. Thanks also to Robert Zabawa at Tuskegee University, who opened his personal library and shared his resources and his time so freely. Special thanks to Kate Epstein, whose clarity and contributions made the writing process much easier.

I am indebted to my colleagues at the University of Wisconsin-Madison, who have been incredibly supportive of my work. There was never a request that you didn't fulfill. I am grateful to work with such brilliant, thoughtful, and giving colleagues. From day one, Paul Robbins of the Gaylord Nelson Institute for Environmental Studies has asked how he could support my work, and he has followed through with every request. Gregg Mitman not only twisted my arm to convince me to come to Madison, but he has provided valuable advice and feedback. Bill Cronon challenged me to think about who I wanted to be as an intellectual and as an activist. Steve Ventura and Margaret Krome offered me love, their cabin, and a meal when the research process became overwhelming. Thank you Nebi Hilliard, Mindi Thompson, Benjamin Ball, Bianca Baldridge, Erica Turner, and all of the members of our writing group who offered regular conversations with lots of laughter and the support I needed to stay the path.

To the members of the Department of Community and Environmental Sociology, thank you for the brown bags and faculty colloquia that you organized that helped me see my way through lots of directions and ideas. Jess Gilbert offered feedback on early drafts, shared intellectual resources, and connected me to people in the South. Jack Kloppenburg helped me find my voice with pointed questions and a loving and supportive hand. Noah Feinstein, you started off as my accountability buddy and have become my friend. Katherine Curtis, LeAnn Tigges, Gary Green, Mike Bell, Randy Stoecker, and Daniel Kleinman, you have supported these ideas from the beginning. Thanks to my colleagues in the

UW-Madison Sociology Department: Pam Oliver, Alice Goffman, and others, who offered feedback on theoretical and methodological approaches. Thanks to colleagues elsewhere who offered suggestions on previous versions of the manuscript and whose work inspired my own: Craig Harris, Michigan State University; David Brunsma, Virginia Tech University; April Mayes, Pomona College; Tanya Golash Boza, University of California, Merced; Kwasi Densu, Florida A&M University; Dorceta Taylor, University of Michigan; Psyche Williams-Forson, University of Maryland; Ashanté Reese, Spelman College; and LaShawnDa Pittman, University of Washington. A special thank you to Jessica Nembhard at the John Jay College of Criminal Justice, who offered support and who demonstrated by example the way to build a narrative using disparate pieces of history to tell a story of freedom. To my research assistants at UW-Madison: Jaclyn Wylper and Isaac Leslie, who have been especially helpful with coding and thinking about the broader implications of this project. You've taken my theoretical framework and made it your own, thank you for your contributions.

Thank you to the photographers who captured the images that tell stories, especially Patricia Gouvdis, Jeremy Brockman, and Franklynn Peterson. Thank you to the archivists and keepers of the organizational documents who provided the data for my research. Those who retain historical documents and records have a special place in the heart of an academic. Thanks to Dana Chandler, archivist at Tuskegee University, and to archivists at the Amistad Collection at Tulane University and the Schomburg Center for Research in Black Culture, Mississippi Department of History, Wisconsin Historical Society, Birmingham Public Library, Alabama State Archives, and the Walter Reuther Archives.

Many farmers have loved me and taught me so much. Thanks to Mr. Ben Burkett, for all of the introductions, for explaining historical and contemporary contexts, for answering all of my questions about the life of a farmer, and for taking me on the long drives between Petal, Mississippi, and Epes, Alabama. You've trusted me with your knowledge, introduced me to fellow farmers, and accepted me as family, and I am forever indebted. Thanks also to Mr. Daniel Teague of the Mississippi Association of Cooperatives, Mr. George and Mrs. Alice Paris, Rev. Wendell Paris, and Mr. John Zippert of the Federation of Southern Cooperatives; Rev. and Mrs. Sherrod of New Communities; and Rev. Jeff and Rev. Sarah Goldstein of Measure for Measure in Madison who shared their memories of Ms. Fannie Lou Hamer.

I couldn't imagine a better team with whom to work than the editors at the University of North Carolina Press. Thanks to Brandon Proia, who consistently encouraged me to write the book that was my own; to Rhonda Williams, who offered so many brilliant suggestions, and who, with Heather Ann Thompson, has created a space for interdisciplinary work on civil rights and black power. Thanks also to the anonymous reviewers.

Jane Collins raised the bar and set the standard for what it means to be a mentor, a colleague, and a friend. As my doula for birthing this project, Jane reminded me to breathe, held my hand, and offered encouragement and endless edits. She was right there with me every step of the way. We've laughed and cried and celebrated together, and through it all, we became sisters. Your thoughtfulness and patience have meant so much to me.

Thank you to my family: my maternal grandparents, Mr. Kenneth Brown and Ms. Bessie Pearl Brown; my paternal grandmother, Ms. Marilyn Triggs; my parents, Dr. Maurice O. White and Maggie B.; and my sister Marilyn, who instilled in me a sense of curiosity about the world, courage, and a challenge to build community in order to make things better than I found them. I'm forever grateful for your introduction to the love of all that is intellectual. And to my partner in life, Anthony J. Sprewer, you have offered me comfort, love, support, a family, and a sense of community. I can never thank you enough for all you've been to me and for all you've done.

Foreword

When I first heard about Monica White's work, I was already looking, as she was, to fill in the blanks in the story of black people's role in food justice that the dominant food movement narrative had left out. I wanted this for myself and for my son, whose birth was the impetus for my own journey into the world of food justice. I thought I was prepared to be the mother of a black boy in the United States. I thought I understood the threats and obstacles that he would face because of his race and gender. I anticipated that he would need a proper education to all the traps that a black boy must maneuver to become a man. I never imagined that the U.S. food and agricultural system would become part of the list of threats to his life, but he is allergic to eggs, peanuts, shellfish, and all dairy products. I wanted him to live free, and I knew that his survival was related to my ability to find out more about the food system. I had a family to feed. I had to do the practical work that would feed my family. Stewardship of urban land was my route to food activism that led to demanding food justice for me, my family, and my community.

Working urban land to feed my son, I had uncovered a connection to the land that I did not expect. I learned that growing food was an act of resistance. This insight is also a central point of the book you hold in your hands. Growing food on the West Side of Chicago, I was excited to learn that there were others, across the country, who were just as concerned about the food system. Yet it became clear very quickly that the predominantly white food movement saw the lack of healthy food in my community as a sign that we did not care for healthy food. Those in that movement blamed culture and poor food choices, not industrial agriculture. The solutions they proposed included food pantries, classes to teach healthy eating, and other remedies that tended to pathologize the culture rather than the food and agricultural industry.

None of the suggestions ever promoted self-sufficiency. Thus, growing food became an act of resistance both to these faulty assumptions and to the system that failed to provide for us.

This book extends that insight. The contributions of people of color and indigenous nations are missing in our understanding of food history. Our legacy has been erased. Manifest Destiny erased the contributions of black and indigenous people to the United States. When I met Monica, I was looking for information that acknowledged and reclaimed the legacy of black people in the founding of the food system in the United States. As a black woman, being able to use another black woman's work to honor the work of black people, and especially black women, is empowering. This book confirms what I knew had to be true: black people have a historical connection to the land in the United States. The land ethic that Monica's work uncovered is our history: our way of being on land, on our own terms with pride and dignity.

Monica's work recognizes that we all must live in the gap between the truth of who we are and who we hope to become. Knowing the history of my people, the blank space in the dominant narrative of the agricultural/food/environmental movement made no sense. While the white food movement describes my community through a deficit model, Monica's work describes agriculture as a site of resistance. In my experience of the white food movement, if food was mentioned, it was to suggest that soul food, the traditional cuisine of African Americans, was unhealthy. When I wanted to convert vacant lots to urban farms, I was told that my community had no real role in the food system besides that of consumer. Researchers called our communities "food deserts" and favored large-scale food retailers as saviors of the community rather than urban agriculture or farmers' markets operated for and by the community. The food movement's narrative made no reference to black Americans' connection to the land, completely omitting the African slave trade and the institution of slavery in its narrative of American agriculture. Outside of that narrative, black people's experience of agriculture has been understood as one of subjugation, hardship, and danger. Without betraying that history, Monica's work provides a counternarrative: one of self-sufficiency, resistance, and a food justice movement that can serve black people.

This book reclaims our historical legacy of cooperation and shows that we can develop economically viable communities. White supremacy drove a wedge between us and our relationship to the land. The terror that our people faced in the past when working the land was real. We need to address the stigma that impacts the descendants of those who were enslaved and the cultural memory of the oppression, exploitation, and trauma of the sharecropping system. The land holds the key to unlocking the shackles of white supremacy. The land holds our healing. This book reminds us of the role of food and farming in the black freedom movement. The activism of the people whose legacy this book recovers was tied to their love of the land. It helps us recognize that our relationship to the land is not just the story of oppression, but one of liberation. Land access and ownership gives us the power to heal ourselves.

Monica's book tells the important stories of the land and the people and the institutions they created in order to resist: George Washington Carver, Tuskegee University, Fannie Lou Hamer, the black agricultural cooperatives of the American South, Detroit's D-Town farmers, as well as many others whose names are lost to history but whose resistance can be recovered in the archives that she painstakingly pieced together. Monica's book tells the story of resistance to oppression by those who stayed close to the land and fed themselves. This vital work in recovering the stories of the surviving members of these movements and their heirs is a healing balm. The black land ethic is alive and well in these pages and in the contemporary urban food movement. By telling the history of our people on this land, Monica has given us all a magnificent gift. In recovering this story, she has revealed the strength, faith, and intelligence of the people who came before us. We stand on strong shoulders. Holding on to the dream of freedom, they understood that the land could set them free. Tending the soil is one thing, but getting it to return life to you is another.

Before this book, I looked for those stories. This work brings them into full view. It fills a tremendous void in our movement, providing a foundation that will reveal what food justice means for black people in the twenty-first century. This book creates a foundation that is needed for the generations to come.

The path to freedom is collective. We cannot do this individually. We need each other. We need our land and our food. Food is culture. The land holds our memories. The dominant white food narrative says that it is important to know where food comes from, who grew it, and who prepared it. However, what's needed is a narrative that connects food and land to our collective struggles and our history as black people. This book is a conduit of those stories and memories that restore our dignity. I hope it will forever remind us that we are people of this land.

LaDonna Redmond
Campaign for Food Justice Now
November 3, 2017

PART I

Land, Food, and Freedom

Black Farmers, Agriculture, and Resistance

> It is pleasant to know that in color, form, and features, we are related to the first successful tillers of the soil; to the people who taught the world agriculture. —Frederick Douglass, 1873

> There is no reason why the Negro should not control the Negro trade and handle the money the Negro has to spend. —Rev. E. F. Love, 1888

Historians, novelists, filmmakers, and persons engaged in casual conversation often tell the story of the relationship between landless African American farmers and the soil as one of oppression and exploitation.[1] Indeed, painful memories attend slavery, tenant farming, sharecropping, and land loss. But this book offers another narrative of the relationship between labor, land use, and the black farmers whose contributions were intrinsic to the development of the agricultural sector of the United States of America. Recent scholarship has begun to describe the important role of black landowners in organizing the civil rights movement, including those who provided lodging, food, and an organizational structure for Freedom Riders, facilitated voting rights organizing, and spearheaded anti-Jim Crow activism.[2] Yet those who worked the land not only supported resistance strategies; they created and employed them. This book recovers the efforts of black landowners as well as the civil rights activism of sharecroppers, tenant farmers, and domestic workers. It focuses its attention on those who refused to migrate and who fought to stay in the South and maintain communities around agriculture. This book is an effort to recover, tell, and honor the stories of collective agency and community resilience of the black rural poor, a group the civil rights movement left behind. Whether they worked the land

3

part-time, as many domestic workers did, or full time; whether they owned land or did not, their connection to southern soil was the basis of their unity.

The term "farmers" in this book's title refers to all those who worked the land, regardless of their landownership status. This includes sharecroppers, tenant farmers, and landowners.[3] In an earlier time, it even included those who were enslaved in rural places. It encompasses subsistence farmers, many of whom were women, who after putting in long hours as domestic workers in rural settings, used their small amounts of free time to perform the gardening and farmwork necessary for survival. Our historical memory has been profoundly affected by those narratives of the civil rights movement that, in emphasizing the "talented tenth," have failed to capture the roles of black working-class men and women and thus often have ignored the legacy of black farmers and those who lived close to the land. This book documents forms of southern rural resistance by which black farmers responded to extreme conditions of repression: how they fought for the right to participate in the food system as producers and to earn a living wage in agriculture in the face of racially, socially, and politically repressive conditions, using land as a strategy to move toward freedom. It focuses on the agricultural cooperatives that these farmers created as the basis for self-reliant and self-determined community. By reclaiming that legacy, this book provides a historical foundation that will add meaning and perspective for the resurgence of agriculture in the context of contemporary food justice/sovereignty movements in the United States, especially in cities such as Detroit, Chicago, Milwaukee, New York, and New Orleans.

The post agricultural society of the Jim Crow South left many black southerners homeless, unemployed, and hungry in the same way that postindustrial societies of the northern United States have left many black factory workers homeless, unemployed, and hungry. Black farmers in the South engaged in agriculture as a way to survive when vast numbers of their peers joined the Great Migrations to the North and West.[4] They pooled their resources in a way that produced a remarkable array of services, providing food, housing, education, employment, childcare, and health care collectively. These are lessons for underserved communities in today's cities that are attempting to identify ways of reorganizing their work, reimagining their communities, and rebuilding their neighborhoods with a commitment to social responsibility and environmental sustainability.

This book illustrates how black agricultural cooperatives—using Freedom Farm Cooperative (FFC), North Bolivar County Farmers Cooperative (NBCFC), the Federation of Southern Cooperatives (FSC) and the Detroit Black Community Food Security Network (DBCFSN) as examples—engaged in community development efforts as a strategy of resistance. It explains how, in response to extreme conditions of financial, social, and political oppression, black farmers created agricultural cooperatives as a space and place to practice freedom. While their experiences with white politicians, landowners, and merchants left them feeling dependent, vulnerable, exploited, and fearful for their very lives, their cooperatives enacted strategies of prefigurative politics, economic autonomy, and commons as praxis. They demonstrated collective agency and community resilience (CACR) in working toward and practicing freedom—freedom to participate in the political process, to engage in an economic model that was cooperative and fair, and to exchange ideas with others who shared their goals. These organizations offered the space to be innovative and practice a liberated community built upon principles of cooperative living and self-sufficiency.

One major objective of this book is to connect contemporary urban farmer-activists to an earlier time when African Americans turned to agriculture as a strategy for building sustainable communities. As an activist and urban ethnographer of the food justice–urban agriculture movement in Detroit since 2007, I have worked with others to transform and rebuild a financially devastated city. Across the generations, black Detroiters are using agriculture as a way to convert vacant lots with overgrown grass into community gardens that serve as social spaces.[5] These spaces now function as community centers where people learn about healthy eating, increase their access to healthy food, and receive health services. They are places where intergenerational relationships are nurtured and maintained and where residents have a safe space for exercise. For many in Detroit, the new relationships they forge between land, food, and freedom are a response to the housing foreclosure crisis, the closing of public schools, the water shut-off crisis, and issues of policing.

Theoretical Framework: Collective Agency and Community Resilience

Collective agency and community resilience (CACR) is a theoretical framework that builds upon and amplifies the social movement concept of everyday strategies of resistance. James Scott and Benedict Kerkvliet use the term "everyday strategies of resistance" to refer to forms of resistance that are often overlooked or overshadowed by a focus on organized social movements. Everyday resistance typically is less confrontational, incurs less repression, and is usually enacted by individuals or small groups. It refers to "what people do . . . that reveals disgust, anger, or opposition to what they regard as unjust or unfair actions by others more wealthy or powerful than they . . . [and] the expressions of people who perceive injustice but for various reasons are unable or unwilling to push improvements in an organized, direct manner."[6]

But even the study of everyday forms of resistance misses activities that are not disruptive but rather constructive, in the sense that the aggrieved actively build alternatives to existing political and economic relationships. The acts of building knowledge, skills, community, and economic independence have a radical potential that the term does not encompass. We might then ask: Is it possible to conceptualize these ways of building self-sufficiency and self-reliance as resistance in their own right?[7]

Offering new feminist, collective, community, and political dimensions, the framework of CACR captures the activities community members enact as a means to be self-reliant and self-sufficient. By recovering these acts of building sustainable communities through alternative community structures, I seek to complement studies of marches, sit-ins, boycotts, and other traditional means of protest with documentation of the alternative community structures that activists have created to meet community needs—whether social, political, or economic. Consistent with grounded theory's concept of theoretical sensitivity,[8] theories of social movements and resistance inform this framework—but CACR organically emerged from my coding and analysis of the archival documents and interviews I collected. Using methods of grounded theory, I constructed the framework as a way to encompass the vision and accomplishments of black farm cooperatives. It is an attempt to represent the congealed wisdom and strategies that inform their efforts.

Collective agency, a concept that I coined based upon the data for this project, involves social actors' ability to create and enact behavioral options necessary to affect their political future. As such, it is an intrinsic part of social activism. How people understand and conceptualize their own agency affects their beliefs about whether they can influence the course of events in their own lives. Based on the information available to them and their interpretation of that information, their sense of agency allows them to make decisions either to resist or adhere to social boundaries. Those who join movements develop a type of agency that includes a willingness to give up the individual rewards granted by the hegemonic power of the social hierarchy and to find rewards in movement participation.

Most scholarship on the concept of agency concentrates on its psychological origins and impact and its implications for the individual. I propose *collective* agency as a way to expand theories of agency to include a collective dimension. A community does not have a consciousness in the same way an individual does, but when a group of people comes together and believes in their mutual success, this creates a separate type of consciousness that drives collective agency. The concept of collective agency provides grounding for this book's investigation of those who share a collective identity and who join together in efforts to create new social forms.

Community resilience, a subcategory within the burgeoning field of resilience science, refers to the various structural aspects and components of human adaptation to extreme adversity, using "community" as the unit of analysis.[9] The theory of community resilience pays particular attention to community-based forms of social organization that plan for and respond to political violence, environmental/climate change, and other forms of natural and human-induced disasters. It concentrates on ways to adjust, withstand, and absorb disturbance, and to reorganize while undergoing change. It emphasizes structural approaches and community engagement, including types of indigenous knowledge, emotional experiences, and intraracial/interracial exchanges that communities need in order to adapt to unforeseen conditions. For example, when a community of farmworkers faces the refusal of local merchants to sell them farm supplies and develops a cooperative to pool their resources to purchase those supplies from national merchants, they demonstrate resilience in the face of a system that benefits from their exploitation and their oppression.

Strategies for Collective Agency and Community Resilience

The communities this book describes enacted CACR using three primary strategies that other theories of resistance have not adequately captured. These are: (1) commons as praxis, (2) prefigurative politics, and (3) economic autonomy. These strategies, while not mutually exclusive, encompass the ideological-social, political, and economic aspects of community reliance and community determination as strategies for freedom and liberation. For example, a single institution such as a Freedom School—a school created to educate black children in the context of Jim Crow laws depriving them of public education—may be economically autonomous, but it may also be a demonstration of prefigurative politics and of commons as praxis.

COMMONS AS PRAXIS

The development of commons as praxis is a critical transition in the ways that members of oppressed communities think and organize. Commons as praxis engages and contests dominant practices of ownership, consumerism, and individualism and replaces them with shared social status and shared identities of race and class. It functions as an organizing strategy that emphasizes community well-being and wellness for the benefit of all. It is based on the premise that pooling resources can transcend the limitations of individual strength in oppressed communities. It emphasizes the shared ideology and the cooperative/collective behaviors that arise in response to the conditions of oppression. Community decisions made around shared spaces and resources such as access to land, water, and seeds are examples of commons as praxis.

PREFIGURATIVE POLITICS

Prefigurative politics refers to the construction of alternative political systems that are democratic and include processes of self-reflection. Also referred to as "everyday utopias,"[10] place-based alternative practices,[11] and alternative experiments in everyday living,[12] prefigurative politics involves several progressive components, including free spaces and democratic representation.

Prefigurative politics begins with the awareness that members of a group have been excluded from the political process. The group responds by developing free spaces to meet without fear of repression to share their grievances and to foster and discuss innovative ideas that will help them move toward freedom and liberation.[13] Free spaces are critical for understanding, interrogating, and engaging democratic and revolutionizing principles that stand in stark contrast to the structures identified as oppressive. Through political education, community members engage in consciousness raising and information exchange, which allows them to think creatively about the current political situation and how they would reconceptualize those arrangements. It allows them to consider alternative ways of engagement with power that include principles of community self-determination and community self-reliance.

At the individual level, prefigurative politics introduces community members to new ideas that encourage new ways of being, along with a greater sense of freedom and independence, and thus create the opportunity to move from conditions of oppression to conditions of self-sufficiency and self-determination. At the community level, the spaces prefigurative politics creates are locations where members of oppressed groups are able to speak freely, strategize, and offer political education and politicization to members of the group; they can move from describing and discussing the conditions of oppression to strategizing and conceptualizing movement toward freedom and liberation. Within these spaces, members engage in democratic practices. Community members create the opportunity to practice democracy, when they have been excluded from it in the rest of the world. Once a community creates and initiates new ways of decision-making and political autonomy, an economically independent and autonomous community becomes apparent and necessary.

ECONOMIC AUTONOMY

Given the economic and racial exploitation in the history of southern agriculture—including structures of sharecropping, tenant farming, and Jim Crow legislation—economic autonomy is a critical dimension of collective agency and community resilience. In response to economic exploitation, and in opposition to a resource extraction model in which all forms of economic participation support the status quo, efforts to establish economic autonomy create an alternative system of resource exchange within the community, and these funds and resources have direct benefits for all of its members.

The pursuit of economic autonomy allowed communities to provide for their members financially and to help them move from dependence to independence and from powerlessness toward a position of power. Economic autonomy often involves creating an alternative economic system, such as replacing the exchange of federal currency with barter of labor or produce. Building economic autonomy thus creates a platform for working to end social, political, and economic oppression. By developing an independent system, a community could begin to extract its members from an oppressive system at the same time that it built capacity through fostering new forms of collective self-governance.

In the South, prior to establishing cooperatives, tenant farmers and sharecroppers often had experiences that left them feeling economically dependent, their labor exploited and themselves discarded. The creation of institutions that enhanced their economic autonomy offered a powerful alternative. Yet economic autonomy is in fact an ideal and is always a matter of degree in a globalized economy. The people who see themselves as economically autonomous in today's world—wealthy Americans, most of them white—in fact depend on a host of factors and government subsidies and, frequently, the labor of those less powerful than themselves to retain their economic power. Thus, the economic autonomy that cooperatives seek is a process, a continuum that moves from complete dependence on an oppressive structure to independence. Arguably, in a global economy, independence is always partial and is extremely difficult to accomplish; however, progress toward it can be leveraged for power and self-determination.

Four Hundred Years of Collective Agency and Community Resilience

SLAVE GARDENS AS RESISTANCE

African American practices of connecting land, food, and freedom have a rich and complex history. While the data for *Freedom Farmers* focuses largely on the Southern Cooperative Movement of the late 1960s through 1974, urban gardens in today's Rust Belt cities can draw on a story that begins in the earliest days of New World slavery. The millions of men, women, and children who were kidnapped from their homelands in Africa and transported through the Middle Passage, in the most extreme case of forced deportation in world history, possessed knowledge of microclimates and the particular kinds of crops that they could grow in the places where they would toil as enslaved. As Judith A. Carney and Richard Nicholas Rosomoff write, this knowledge tells a story: "African food staples were pioneered [in the Americas and the Caribbean] by enslaved, underfed Africans who faced in the early colonial period the real prospect of starvation. In their struggle to stay alive, enslaved Africans drew deeply upon the agricultural expertise and the crops of their own heritage, while adopting the knowledge systems and plants bequeathed to them by Amerindians. Through this new assembly of tropical food plants, we grasp in part the remarkable efforts they made to stay alive in the face of despair and unimaginable toil."[14]

In addition to human cargo, slave ships carried African food staples, seeds, root vegetables, other produce, and livestock. These staples would feed the crew and, minimally, the enslaved, but they were also incorporated into the agriculture of plantation economies and became critical to the survival and well-being of both those living in slavery and their captors. Researchers identify the introduction of African yams, arrowroot, bananas, various types of beans, cowpeas, eddo, guinea squash, hibiscus, lablab beans, millet, okra, pearl millet, pigeon peas, plantains, purslane, rice, sesame, sorghum, sweet potatoes, tamarind, taro, and watermelon to the Americas and the Caribbean through the Middle Passage.

Through their knowledge of African crops and their agricultural prowess, enslaved Africans supported the development of cash crops and commodities such as sugar, coffee, chocolate, and rice, as well as subsistence crops. As Carney and Rosomoff argue, colonizers were tradespeople, not farmers; they had little experience growing food, and thus their survival depended on the knowledge of those who lived in slavery.[15] Working collaboratively with indigenous peoples, enslaved Africans provided the skills to feed the inhabitants of the Americas.

Using oral traditions of storytelling, Carney collected many stories about an enslaved African woman who carried the seeds of rice in her hair, unbeknownst to her captors.[16] Thus, the introduction of crops and livestock was not only a strategy of survival; it was also a strategy of resistance. Those who were enslaved credited this revolutionary act of transoceanic seed transfer with saving their lives and those of their descendants—forming the foundation for the South Carolina rice economy, for which the region would become internationally recognized.

Archaeologists, ethnobotanists, geographers, and historians who study plantation agriculture and slavery in the United States describe a variety of strategies that enslaved individuals used to ensure their own food supply and nutrition. White enslavers typically disbursed and distributed food based on enslaved peoples' capacity to provide labor. In other words, those who worked the hardest and produced the most received more and better food. For many, it was not enough. They foraged native wild edibles, hunted, fished, grew their own food in gardens, or raised livestock. As Carney and Rosomoff found, food strategies blended with health strategies, as enslaved black laborers identified and used as many as six hundred species of medicinal plants.[17]

Scholars have identified the location of slave gardens, or provision/kitchen grounds, on many former plantations, including the remnants of African seed and root crops that eventually made their way into the diets of contemporary Americans. Most likely working on Saturday or Sunday, those who were enslaved grew crops such as various types of squash, yams, sweet potatoes, various kinds of peas (such as guinea peas from New Guinea), and, for soil fertility and ceremonial purposes, cow and pigeon peas.[18]

The status of these gardens in the functioning of the plantation is the subject of some scholarly debate. Enslavers clearly realized some benefit from these gardens, as the enslaved could not work without food. B. J. Barickman suggests that those who were enslaved planned and tended these gardens after long, arduous labor under the same implicit threat that characterized their labor in the fields.[19] Yet it seems likely that enslaved people decided what to grow, how to grow it, and what to do with the harvest in these gardens. Thus, slave gardens represented independent production grounds and can be understood as a strategy of resistance to a corrupt system and an effort to create food security. Dale W. Tomich argues that enslaved people created markets to barter, exchange, and sell their produce among themselves and others.[20] If they earned cash in such markets, they might even purchase their freedom. Some documented cases have found that enslavers respected the enslaved's ownership of such produce to the extent of paying for it. Barickman acknowledges the existence of "an extensive and even impressive range of independent production and marketing activities."[21] Thus, food provisioning can be seen as liberatory; enslaved peoples used food production as a strategy of developing social relations and some autonomy.[22] For those who were enslaved, this practice of growing food, especially foods from the mother-land, and the social exchanges that went on in the marketplaces were also opportunities to enact freedom. Using food production, the enslaved were able to practice the cultural and ceremonial uses of land they had brought with them, as a way to celebrate their ancestors and the homeland they left behind.

Examples of black farming as resistance occurred during the transition from slavery to Reconstruction and well into the Jim Crow era. Under Jim Crow, certain black communities were known as black settlement towns, freedom villages, freedmen's settlements, or freedom colonies. Those emancipated from slavery and their offspring joined these intentional communities or communes to avoid and resist the exploitative conditions of sharecropping and tenant farming systems, often by settling on unclaimed land and building successful family farms in communities. An extensive body of scholarship documents the ways that these all-black towns escaped the exploitative and oppressive conditions of slavery or Jim Crow.[23] In the 1960s, after plantation owners put tenant farmers and sharecroppers off their land for demanding higher wages, and in an effort to stop them from organizing, black farmers founded "Strike Town" and "Freedom Town," both in Mississippi.[24]

THE COLORED FARMERS ALLIANCE

The Colored Farmers National Alliance and Cooperative Union, also known as the Colored Farmers Alliance (CFA), was a precursor to the cooperatives on which this book focuses.[25] Formed in 1886 in Texas, the most conservative measures put its membership at 1.2 million and its reach at 175 chapters throughout the South, with representation in every southern state. Virtually all of CFA's members were black. Each chapter had elected officers such as president, vice-president, treasurer, secretary, and superintendent; there were also positions such as conductor, lecturer, chaplain, and doorkeeper. CFA engaged in conventional political protest activities against monopolistic business practices, encouraging independent coalitions of black farmers to represent their interests as landless workers and running their own candidates for political office.[26] Its members engaged in disruptive strategies that included harvest strikes and economic boycotts. For example, in 1886, the Black Knights, an affiliate of CFA, called for a cotton pickers' strike in Arkansas.[27] They also exhibited collective agency by pooling their resources to purchase land and tools and to offer loans and increase the options for black farmworkers. CFA created regional trading posts and membership exchange locations in Houston, New Orleans, Mobile, Charleston, and Norfolk, Virginia, for the purchase and distribution of farm supplies and staple crops.

CFA members demonstrated the strategy of commons as praxis in their self-governance and in their creation of cultural cues and shared information and knowledge. In one example, members of CFA created a secret language, with passwords, a member handshake, greetings, and attire for specific occasions. In addition to paying dues, members purchased organizational badges and other regalia that identified their affiliation. These rituals of solidarity provided a platform for collective economic behavior, and members frequently pooled resources for such objectives as purchasing farm supplies.

CFA ceased to exist five years after it was created. Repression from those in power and violence against its members after a poorly managed harvest strike in 1891 caused the organization's demise. The model it pioneered, however, and the collective and cooperative dimensions it established as modes of resistance would have power into the next century. The chapters that follow examine agricultural cooperatives that followed CFA's model, demonstrating its power and resilience in later incarnations.

THE UNIVERSAL NEGRO IMPROVEMENT ASSOCIATION

The efforts of Marcus Garvey that began in 1915 with a letter to Booker T. Washington also prefigured the cooperative movement on which this book focuses.[28] Garvey, a native of Jamaica, was planning to build an industrial farm and educational institute in Jamaica on the model of Tuskegee Institute. He sought Washington's help in planning a series of lectures he would deliver across the United States to raise funds for the venture. Subscribing to the ideals of black nationalism, pan-Africanism, self-determination, and self-reliance as a means to develop political and economic autonomy, Garvey envisioned industrial education as a strategy toward freedom. He admired Washington's emphasis and attention to industrial education as well as his fund-raising for Tuskegee and its development as a black-owned educational system.

Garvey's objective was to provide educational opportunities, training, and reintegration to build a self-sufficient, self-determined community, with agriculture at its foundation. One group Garvey intended to target was the formerly incarcerated. In Garvey's vision, the farm would change not only the fate of individuals who received training but the moral and industrial condition of the country.[29] As he wrote to Washington, he saw agriculture as a way to "teach our people on the objects of race pride, race development, and other useful subjects."[30]

Garvey realized aspects of his vision in the Universal Negro Improvement Association (UNIA) in 1914. The UNIA had seven hundred branches in thirty-eight states and four million members by the early 1920s, reaching from Africa to throughout the African diaspora, including the Americas and the Caribbean.[31] The UNIA established Liberty Farm in Oregonia, Ohio, around 1945.[32] Little information survives about its accomplishments. Garvey died at the age of fifty-two in 1940, and James R. Stewart of Cleveland succeeded him as the leader of UNIA. While the organization never realized Garvey's agricultural goals to the extent he envisioned, self-sufficiency through food production remained a significant theme in its understanding of itself and its mission to free black people throughout the world.

FOOD AND AGRICULTURE IN THE CIVIL RIGHTS AND BLACK POWER MOVEMENTS

During the civil rights movement, African Americans organized to seek access to and fully participate in education, politics, and public resources. Individuals in urban areas made advances on each of these levels. However, a less well-known aspect of the movement was its antipoverty agenda. Following the 1963 March on Washington, the Southern Christian Leadership Conference

(SCLC) organized the Poor People's Campaign, an effort to alleviate poverty for all Americans.[33]

Under the leadership of Martin Luther King Jr., the SCLC recognized the relationship between race and poverty as well as the special relationship of African Americans to the land. In a little-referenced speech, King pointed out that the U.S. government's decision not to honor the promise of "forty acres and a mule" to freed men and women coincided with its bestowal of millions of acres of land (stolen from native peoples) on white people in the West and Midwest. He described the government's provision of state-funded land grant colleges that taught poor whites how to farm, of county agents with expertise in farming, and of financial support in the form of grants and low-interest loans. Further, King noted, "many [white farmers] are receiving millions of dollars in federal subsidies not to farm and they are the very people telling the Black man that he ought to lift himself by his own bootstraps. This is what we are faced with and this is a reality. Now, when we come to Washington in this campaign, we're coming to get our check."[34]

Thus, King demonstrated his understanding of how a broken relationship to the land fostered poverty among African Americans and how racial injustice structured relationships between education, landownership, labor, and poverty. King was not alone in recognizing the centrality of agriculture to the black experience. The Black Power movement also acknowledged this history. Malcolm X suggested that the goal of revolution was integrally related to access to land: "A revolution is based on land. Land is the basis of all independence. Land is the basis of freedom, justice and equality. . . . It's based on land. A revolutionary wants land so he can set up his own nation, an independent nation."[35]

Black Power organizations such as the Black Panther Party (BPP) emphasized the importance of access to and affordability of healthy food. They also recognized the importance of landownership, of supporting rural black farmers, and the critical role of southern agriculture in feeding urban populations of African Americans. Admonitions such as the Republic of New Afrika's slogan "Free the

Land!" reflected a demand for African Americans to reclaim their connection to land as a strategy for black political development and for liberation and freedom.

The BPP created survival programs to provide nutrition in response to hunger in the black community in the 1960s, demonstrating an understanding of the importance of nutrition to the cause of freedom.[36] This was manifest in programs such as free breakfast for children (over twenty-two chapters fed twenty thousand children at the height of the program),[37] liberation schools, medical clinics (which provided house calls),[38] childcare centers, clothing programs, and political education. Through such programs, the activists of the BPP emphasized their desire to build a well-fed, well-cared for, healthy black community. BPP cofounder Huey Newton wrote that the organization was founded "to develop a lifeline to the people by serving their needs and defending them against their oppressors." He continued: "We knew that this strategy would raise the consciousness of the people and [that they would] give us their support."[39]

The free breakfast program was arguably the most successful of the BPP's efforts to meet the needs of the community, but the free grocery programs also fed many. Using food as an organizing strategy pointed to the failure of the federal government to care for its citizens. More importantly, it showed the power of the people and the ways that collective social responsibility could provide what a community needs to be healthy, whole, and liberated.

The Nation of Islam (NOI) also employed food justice strategies to provide access to healthy food in many urban centers where they were active. In the late 1960s, the organization owned approximately 13,000 acres throughout the South, collectively called Salaam Agricultural Systems. This ambitious undertaking included 4,200 acres in Georgia, 5,000 acres in Morengo County, Alabama, and 4,000 acres in Greene County, Alabama.[40] While the assassination of Malcolm X brought decline and forced the division and dissolution of assets, the Nation of Islam returned to agricultural endeavors in 1994, creating Muhammad Farms on 1,556 acres in rural South Georgia. In addition to producing livestock cared for using organic practices, NOI produced substantial quantities of crops to be shipped to northern cities with large African American populations. The NOI operated restaurants and grocery stores strategically located in these cities.[41]

These varied attempts to place agriculture at the center of a strategy for political development were not ad hoc and piecemeal. They had a strong theoretical basis within the black community. As chapter 2 demonstrates, the scholarship of Booker T. Washington, George Washington Carver, and W. E. B. Du Bois provided ways of thinking that spurred programs such as those of the UNIA, NOI, and BPP. These same patterns spurred the creation of the agricultural cooperatives on which chapters 3, 4, and 5 focus. Booker T. Washington emphasized agriculture as central to community development. He created an economic and educational model for building community-based institutions, specifically for southern black farmers, as a strategy for political participation and inclusion. George Washington Carver's scholarship as an agricultural scientist complemented his commitment to improving the growing strategies of southern black farmers and their ability to create more sustainable agriculture. W. E. B. Du Bois—effectively the United States' first rural sociologist—extensively documented and vividly described the experiences of southern black farmers, especially those who worked as sharecroppers and tenant farmers in Lowndes County, Alabama. He called for the development of cooperatives and collectives as an economic strategy against extreme poverty in the nation's Black Belt in the 1930s. He discussed the ways that farming can become a complex strategy of resistance, one that in some cases confronts structures of oppression while in other cases supports community self-determination.

Methods

In researching this book, I have sought to embody the African principle of *sankofa*: studying the past to understand the present and, from that, to forge a future of our own making. I sought to use a set of research skills to respond to a question that community members, gardeners, farmers, civil rights and human rights activists, food justice activists, and those engaged in the process of rebuilding communities by returning to their agricultural roots would find useful for their work. I also set out to unearth a beautiful and rich history of black farmers and farming, one that documents the centuries of dedicated laborers and their work. I wanted to capture their stories and the ways that they connected work in the fields to their commitment to civil and human rights through developing communities, using a reconnection to the earth as their ally. It was my hope that these historical examples could offer lessons, examples, successes, and failures for contemporary black gardeners, farmers, and food justice advocates who sought a historical framework with which to capture the broader reasons for their work.

To achieve these aims, I needed a methodological approach that would honor both the community-embeddedness of the project and the unconventional nature of my endeavor. Every phase of the project included interacting and engaging with the history and the experiences of those who lived it. This offered me the opportunity to test the applicability and reliability of emerging concepts, themes, ideas, and principles. It was this process that led to a theoretical framework for understanding black community development with agriculture at its center, as a strategy of resistance and a way to build sustainable communities that accepts and allows for the contributions of all members. The way I developed that methodology and conducted the research is a story in itself.

As a faculty member at Wayne State University in my hometown of Detroit from 2005 to 2012, I witnessed an enormous resurgence of urban agriculture in the city. Given that Detroit has a majority black population, I was particularly moved by those initiatives led by black and brown urban farmers descended from migrants from southern states who had sought better living conditions through work in the automobile industry even as they retained a historical connection to agriculture. Most of my own family members are gardeners, so I strongly sympathized with this movement and recognized its deep connection to Detroit history: Detroit passed the first urban ordinance in 1893 that allowed the city's impoverished and food-insecure residents, mostly Irish immigrants, to grow subsistence crops for themselves and their families on undeveloped land. Whereas most locations for 4-H were rural, agricultural communities, Detroit had one of the first urban 4-H clubs. Yet organizations dedicated to the contemporary urban agricultural movement recognized almost none of the black and brown faces of the people I knew and loved who were involved in growing food. Media images of the urban farming movement throughout the nation also excluded these black and brown voices and faces. At the same time, it presented images of those responsible for leading Detroit into the future, such as the owners of home mortgage companies, barbecue restaurants and bakeries, who were also white. Reacting to this marginalization, I began to examine the stories of black Detroiters involved in urban farming to understand why and how they were returning to their agricultural roots and transforming the overgrown lots of weeds and grass into sites of food production, health provision, medical/native plant walks, exercise, public arts, and intergenerational community centers, also called urban gardens.[42]

In 2007, I attended my first meeting of the Detroit Black Community Food Security Network (DBCFSN), an organization that seeks to create self-reliance, food security, and justice in Detroit's black community. At that meeting, the organization's founder and chairperson, Baba Malik Yakini, described the Ujamaa Cooperative Buying Club, which sells the organization's products and organizes cooperative purchases.[43] On its surface, the buying club is a way to purchase healthy foods, health supplements, and household items at a reduced price, but it is also a lesson in cooperation, an experiment in pooling community resources, and a chance to buy together, to work together, and to build together in the direction of justice.

At this time, I had heard of cooperatives, especially in Detroit, but not about their use and function as a part of the black freedom struggle. The decline of U.S. auto production had hit black families in Detroit harder than white families. The jobs left, schools and grocery stores closed, homes were in foreclosure, city services were often neglected, and families were forced to find solutions outside of the market economy. I learned that there were other black urban movements around the nation engaged in developing cooperatives or creating gardens and farms—that is, building organizations around the importance of food and the capacity of food to build community. I learned about food security and its relationship to sovereignty as I began to piece together the vision for building a sustainable community using food as an instrument. DBCFSN's work was a demonstration of collective agency and community resilience, but I did not yet have the theory to understand or explain it.

Given the solution that members of DBCFSN have identified—using agriculture to rebuild a community in response to the economic crisis that the black community experienced—I began to wonder whether black folk had turned to agriculture as a strategy for building sustainable communities in the past. As I began to conduct research, the Colored Farmers Alliance was my first subject. Broadening my search, I journeyed to the South to scour the archives. As I read about black farmers' organizations through four hundred years of history, I kept a running list of all of the black agricultural cooperatives they referenced. I began to travel more and more to seek out organizations' papers and documents.

Freedom Farmers draws its primary data from the documents and records of the North Bolivar County Farmers Cooperative, the Federation of Southern Cooperatives, and Freedom Farm Cooperative. I analyze their leaders' speeches, transcripts of interviews, and photographs. The archives contain material that allowed me to reconstruct these organizations' efforts in building communities and institutions, sharing resources, and participating in the political system. I also used mainstream and African American newspaper articles written at the time of these cooperatives' existence for supplemental and contextual information.

The first archive I visited was at Tuskegee University—specifically, the Booker T. Washington and the George Washington Carver collections. I also traveled to the Alabama Department of Archives and History in Montgomery. The Birmingham Public Library housed the collection of microfilm and microfiche of local, regional, and national newspapers of various agricultural cooperatives. I traveled to the Mississippi Department of Archives and History in Jackson to examine the Fannie Lou Hamer collection and to Tulane University for the Amistad Research Collection that houses both the Fannie Lou Hamer papers and those of the Federation of Southern Cooperatives, especially those donated by John Zippert, cofounder of FSC. The Wisconsin State Historical Society has an extensive civil rights collection, as well as the North Bolivar County Farmers Cooperative records and Fannie Lou Hamer's correspondence with the Madison-based, philanthropic organization Measure for Measure. The Schomburg Center for Research in Black Culture in New York houses the papers of the Interreligious Foundation for Community Organization, which contains documentation of fund-raising for Fannie Lou Hamer's Freedom Farm Cooperative as well as the National Council of Negro Women's annual reviews of FFC. The meticulous records of FSC of its four-decade history were a boon to this project.

Particularly in the South, I visited the archives during the day, but in the evenings I spent time with the black farmers of Mississippi, Alabama, and Georgia, including many who had been active participants in the civil rights movement. We enjoyed tailgating from the back of a pickup truck, sometimes drinking bourbon, as they told me the stories of what they knew, how they knew it, and what they thought it meant for the present day. My meetings were largely informal, but some groups asked me to make presentations on what I found. These conversations provided essential contextualization for what I was reading, and they added depth, as many individuals had memories of the events in question and shared (sometimes divergent) opinions about them. I determined that interviews would be vital for my unfolding research.

From the beginning of this project in 2007 to the present, I have attended countless farm tours as well as conferences for black farmers and conferences on cooperative development, food justice, and developing food hubs. I also visited Cuba to learn about similar urban agricultural cooperatives and community wellness projects there. Conferences provided an invaluable way to locate the individuals who could tell me more, from their own experience, about the black cooperative movement. Several of these conferences specifically addressed agriculture as a strategy to increase access to healthy food in predominantly black neighborhoods. One especially memorable event was the Professional

Agricultural Workers Conference at Tuskegee University (an organization and conference started by Booker T. Washington). In this conference, I learned about techniques to maximize production, harvest purple hull peas, package clams, process crops, and erect irrigation systems, as well as other strategies to move crops from field to market. Meetings like this helped me to capture some of the technical knowledge and specialized language that grounds black agriculture. As a result of connections made at national conferences, I was able to set up semistructured interviews with independent black family farmers, many of whom were also with civil rights activists in southern states who fought for the right to vote among sharecroppers and tenant farmers.

When I attended a Kellogg Foundation conference in Asheville, North Carolina, Shirley Sherrod, a former director of rural development for the U.S. Department of Agriculture, and her husband, Rev. Charles Sherrod, exited the elevator in my hotel just as I was going up to my room. Knowing of their long-term commitment to civil rights and organizing black farmers, and of their dedication to identifying strategies in response to poverty, I had long dreamed of meeting them. The Sherrods were among the founders of New Communities, the first U.S.-based community land trust and the largest land trust owned by African Americans.[44] They purchased almost five thousand acres in Lee County near Albany, Georgia, enacting a vision that included schools, hospitals, markets, and other resources that an independent, self-sufficient black community would require. The Sherrods were very gracious, and we set up a meeting so I could learn about their experiences. This was only one of many connections that my participation at conferences facilitated.

After I joined the faculty of the University of Wisconsin–Madison in 2012, my colleague Jess Gilbert introduced me to Robert Zabawa, research professor of agricultural and resource economics at Tuskegee University. Zabawa took me to explore some of the buildings that still exist from the Prairie Farms Resettlement community that started in the mid-1930s as part of the New Deal and efforts to restore land to landless farmers. These efforts were largely inspired by Booker T. Washington and Tuskegee Institute (now

Tuskegee University), which has provided many resources for the community over the years. Zabawa offered me thousands of pages of precious documents that he had collected through his many visits to the archives for his own research projects. He also introduced me to early leaders of the FSC, Alice and George Paris, and they connected me with George's brother Wendell Paris.

Connections to key individuals sometimes developed in other ways. On another memorable visit south, I was interviewing Wendell Paris at the Federation of Southern Cooperatives training center in Epes, Alabama. In describing the importance of the organization and its beginnings, he told me that white people in the community would often say (in explaining how the dominant culture treats black people's production and purchasing power), "Don't sell a black man a pickup truck; he'll use that to make some money and buy all of the land in Sumpter County. Sell him a Cadillac."[45] At that very moment, Ben Burkett drove up in a silver pickup truck with a bed full of sweet potatoes that he had grown along with other members of the Indian River Springs Cooperative in Petal, Mississippi. In addition to being a fourth-generation farmer, Burkett is a farmer's farmer. He knows almost every small family farmer within a several state radius. He spent countless hours driving me through Alabama and Mississippi, introducing me to black farmers who were cooperative members and civil rights activists in the 1960s and '70s. He answered my questions thoughtfully if he could; if he could not, he connected me with someone who could. We traveled the South on black farmers' tours, and he introduced me to other black Mississippi farmers whose families had been on their land for generations, such as Jesse Fleming and Daniel Teague, who have been deeply committed to growing food and living on the land.

Being in the South also gave me an opportunity to develop a sense of the site where the cooperatives were launched. During one of my trips to Mississippi, I went to Fannie Lou Hamer's home and to her final resting place as a way to get a more tangible sense of her life and the context in which she had launched her bold experiment of Freedom Farm Cooperative. Mindful of the violence perpetrated in Mississippi against African Americans, I ventured to Money, Mississippi, to view the storefront where in 1955 Emmett

Till was accused of "inappropriate behavior" with a white woman, an incident that led to his abduction and brutal murder. This event is said to have spurred the Mississippi civil rights movement.[46]

My experiences in connecting with networks of individuals who had participated in earlier moments of the black cooperative experience were not limited to the South, however. In 2014, I learned that two Madison residents, Jeff and Sarah Goldstein, were directly connected to Fannie Lou Hamer's efforts through Measure for Measure, a Madison-based philanthropic organization that had supported Freedom Farm Cooperative and North Bolivar County Farmers Cooperative for several years. I invited them to attend a presentation that I was giving on FFC at UW-Madison. Jeff told me of his first meeting with Hamer, which took place in the Goldsteins' living room, and about Measure for Measure's work to organize donation drives to provide funding, clothing, books, school supplies, even sewing machines for the sewing cooperatives. He vividly described for me members of Measure for Measure loading these supplies into his car and driving them down to Ruleville, Mississippi.

A Labor of Love

Like others before me, I believe that writing is a labor of love. There are times when writing is difficult, when the words are hard to retrieve and the emotion is palpable. But to me the product feels like love—never easy, but worth it. This book is a love letter. From my first meeting at DBCFSN, I recognized the passion of food justice activists and their efforts to create a community-based food system as a strategy toward liberation. Their children and their excitement on the farm moved me. Watching them reconnecting with the land and playing with worms touched me deeply. For black farmers, the work has always been hard, the days long, and the battles to stay on the land many. Yet black farmers remain committed to growing food and sharing their agricultural and environmental knowledge. I felt love for the members of the food movement who wanted to make sure that children—their own and others in the community—had alternatives to overprocessed, oversalted, and oversugared foods. They had dedicated themselves to providing access to fresh produce, safe places to play, clean water, and a quality education. I felt love for the centuries of black farmers whose labor on the farm sent their children to schools so that they might have a better life than their parents and who built churches and other institutions critical to black community development on their land. I felt love for my own family members: my father, who always grew food and enjoyed cooking for others, and my maternal grandparents who co-owned a community store with local farmers in Eden, North Carolina. That store stood out as the place where African American neighbors were able to purchase farm goods and foodstuffs in the neighborhood from people who respected them.

It is my firm belief that love and research are not at odds, but that the best research is driven by passionate commitment. In this case, as in many others, a loving commitment to a community led to the cocreation of a research question and to a process of discovery that was shaped by the knowledge of black farmers and food justice activists as they worked to transform their communities. What felt at times like serendipity in the research process was often the result of older, wiser members of the community guiding me in my search and connecting me to people and to resources I had not yet discovered. I hope they find this book an adequate reflection of the lessons I learned from them and that it will speak to the next generation seeking empowerment through cultivating the land.

1

Intellectual Traditions in Black Agriculture

Booker T. Washington, George Washington Carver,

and W. E. B. Du Bois

The end of plantation agriculture did not signal a move away from agricultural work for many African Americans. In 1875, African Americans owned three million acres of land. Five years later, they owned eight million, and by 1900, it was twelve million.[1] Agriculture remained an important industry for African Americans. After slavery, many transitioned to sharecropping and tenant farming; a smaller percentage became landowners.[2]

The nation's "race men" recognized the significance and importance of agriculture to the survival and strategies for freedom of African Americans. These were the men who devoted their efforts, intellect, scholarship, public personas, platforms, and resources to advance the interests of African Americans. The most influential and famous—though at times controversial—of the late nineteenth century and early twentieth century were Booker T. Washington, George Washington Carver, and W. E. B. Du Bois. While renowned for a wide array of accomplishments, these men did considerable work on agriculture as central to wellness and as a way to build community. All three men committed their skills to the needs, education, and investigation of black agriculture and/or black farmers. Working in and with communities, they developed theoretical and applied instruments for black community building as resistance in ways that are consistent with a theoretical framework of collective agency and community resilience. This chapter addresses Booker T. Washington's work in building institutional resources for farmers, Carver's efforts in producing, systematizing, and disseminating agricultural knowledge, and Du Bois's efforts to build black community processes, including his advocacy of agricultural cooperatives as an economic and political strategy. For each of these men, in separate ways, agriculture was a strategy of resistance.

Booker T. Washington: Building Institutional Resources

Booker T. Washington was born into slavery in 1856, a decade before Du Bois and Carver. He experienced the nation's transition from plantation agriculture and slavery in a way they did not. Washington is one the most controversial of the race men I discuss here. His emphasis on assimilation, acquiescence, conciliation, and cooperation with white Americans, even in the face of the exploitative and oppressive conditions that followed plantation slavery, has not worn well. His attention to respectability politics—morality, cleanliness, and appearance—and his negative statements about African American farmers do not endear him to modern readers. Washington failed to demand social change or to criticize white southerners for their attempts to maintain as many of the conditions of slavery as possible. His call for recognition of the critical nature of vocational and industrial education as the place where African Americans should concentrate their efforts has been criticized as part and parcel of these elements of his behavior and belief. Yet his contributions to black farmers through agricultural education and extension services were significant, and his legacy is more mixed than contemporary historians have allowed.

The disparaging comments Washington made about those who were recently emancipated and then crushed under racism's boot are painful to read. He criticized their lack of educational attainment, their "ignorance," and their personal habits. In other words, he criticized the situation of people thrust into self-reliance without resources, rather than the structures that oppressed them. Nonetheless, his contributions to black community building were enormous and unprecedented. His work helped millions of black farmers and created the capacity for autonomous agrarian community through building institutions, developing agricultural extension services, and facilitating and organizing black farmers' conferences. However fraught his legacy, it is impossible to tell the story of black agriculture as a site of collective agency and community resilience without considering Washington's work.

THE FOUNDING OF TUSKEGEE

Booker T. Washington regularly affirmed the importance of agriculture in African American life. A typical statement appears in *Working with the Hands,* his second memoir: "It is my conviction that the Negro population must live in the future as they have done in the past, by the cultivation of the soil, and the most helpful service now to be done is to enable the race to follow agriculture with intelligence and diligence."[3]

In his signature achievement, Washington founded the Tuskegee Normal and Industrial Institute (now Tuskegee University) in 1881. He believed that agricultural skills would provide a critical economic source for African American self-sufficiency and community building. Washington wanted to develop an institution committed to providing educational and financial resources for those who experienced severe and abject poverty.

The nature of the education Tuskegee would provide was hotly debated and contested. Washington believed fervently that industrial education was a strategy to garner economic self-reliance. In a piece written in 1903, he declared, "All races that have got upon their feet and remained there have done so largely by laying an economic foundation and by beginning in a proper cultivation and ownership of the soil."[4] At that time, many African Americans had agricultural skills. They were also largely illiterate, which required Washington to develop novel ways to convey the techniques and skills that Tuskegee offered.

Washington's disagreement with Du Bois about industrial and agricultural education is legendary.[5] Du Bois endorsed the idea of educating the "talented tenth" and believed that Tuskegee would consign African Americans to a life of subservience. Washington disagreed: "I plead for industrial education and development for the Negro not because I want to cramp him, but because I want to free him."[6]

Both Du Bois and Washington used a language of racial uplift and racial advancement based on education. But while Du Bois's early work emphasized the talented tenth, Washington's work built institutions and resources and offered recommendations for a larger proportion of African Americans. In keeping with the idea that he could serve the majority of African Americans, he sought to learn about them. He conducted an ethnographic field study of the rural South in the months preceding Tuskegee's opening, traveling by horse and buggy from farm to farm through the Alabama Black Belt, staying with families he met along the way. He used this research to determine the community's needs in order to serve its residents. In his own words, "From the first, I resolved to make the school a real part of the community in which it was located. I was determined that no one should have the feeling that it was a foreign institution, dropped down in the midst of the people."[7]

While the Black Belt originally took its name from the richness of the soil, the term certainly ultimately had racial implications, as African Americans far outnumbered whites in the region.[8] Washington spent months traveling the Black Belt, interviewing and observing black farmers and their families, and taking note of their needs, experiences, and realities. The communities he visited suffered from poverty, peonage, soil depletion, substandard living conditions, and poor agricultural methods. Quality farming equipment was prohibitively expensive, and most black farmers lacked up-to-date tools. Cotton, long the mainstay of farmers in the region, was in decline. Profit margins were either nonexistent or razor thin.

Washington's conclusion based on his fieldwork was unequivocal: "Any people who could see so clearly into their own condition and describe their own condition so vividly as can the common farming class of colored people in the South, could be led a great deal towards their own elevation."[9]

Washington designed Tuskegee's curriculum around his observations. The school provided vocational education courses in construction and other skilled trades such as masonry and carpentry, as well as courses in English, math, and other more standard elements of curriculum. The field research undertaken by

Washington was the foundation for Tuskegee's outreach programs, including the institution's annual Negro farmer's conferences and the moveable schools, for which the institution was celebrated.

Tuskegee was established in the Black Belt's heart in Macon County, Alabama. The campus consisted of a hundred acres of an abandoned plantation, and the first class of thirty students met in 1881, using the existing church structure on the property as their classroom. With "one hoe and a blind mule,"[10] Washington committed himself to building an educational institution that would meet the needs not only of the "sons and daughters of farmers," but also provide educational and agricultural resources to their families who worked and toiled "in the field."[11] In articulating his philosophy in creating the curriculum, Washington said that the curricular "subject matter should complement and originate in the lived experiences of the student."[12] By 1903, the school offered courses and certification in thirty-three different trades, including agriculture, horticulture, dairying, and livestock.[13] Tuskegee operated two farms, and students worked the farms as part of paying tuition.

Agricultural instruction split off from the other trades in 1896, enrolling 325 students in the first year. But even trade students worked on the school's subsistence farm. Washington felt that this was necessary to make all Tuskegee alumni self-sufficient. The school as a whole was built on a model of self-sufficiency and self-reliance. Students in the carpentry classes built the school's furniture. They also built many of the school's buildings. As Washington wrote in 1903, "Of the sixty buildings belonging to the school all but four were almost wholly erected by the students as a part of their industrial education. Even the bricks which go into the walls are made by students in the school's brickyard, in which, last year, they manufactured two million bricks."[14]

Washington thought that farmers knew too little about growing subsistence, or food crops. Most of their knowledge pertained to cash crops such as cotton, corn, and tobacco. He had found fruits and vegetables to be scarce in the diets of the people he visited. Washington made the case for family gardens in his first memoir,

Up from Slavery. Accordingly, Tuskegee students raised food for themselves and to feed livestock, at first on a few acres in 1882 but on 2,300 acres by 1915.[15] These crops soon fed the local community as well, as Tuskegee produce was sold locally and milk produced at the Institute's dairy farm was delivered to local families. The school also provided stud animals to county farmers.

Washington's service to black farmers and their families went beyond campus borders. He acknowledged the generational implications of Tuskegee: "It is not enough to get the sons and daughters into the Institute and teach them useful trades and give them object lessons in good farming: something must be done for the fathers and mothers who cannot come to school."[16]

Programs for the community included state and county fairs; weekly mothers' meetings; farm demonstration work; the Farmers' Monthly Institute, which taught farming techniques to the community; and a "short course" in agriculture designed to provide continuing education to farmers. In addition, Washington recognized the need for farmers to access capital to pay for labor and to purchase land, tools, and seeds. He opened the Tuskegee Savings Department to make loans available to black farmers. Whereas white-owned banks discriminated against black farmers, Washington gave them a chance.[17]

Washington envisioned Tuskegee as a means to lift up the African American community through its alumni. In a speech in 1897, during the dedication of the Armstrong-Slater Memorial Agricultural Building, he articulated his directive to them: "Learn how to achieve practical results in this line of work, and go out and emancipate the less fortunate ones of the race, who still cling to the broken down plow and the half-fed mule and the little patch of half-cultivated cotton."[18] Indeed, alumni took their Tuskegee degrees home, purchased land, and founded many institutes that provided a Tuskegee-based model of education. Tuskegee alumni started schools in Kansas, South Carolina, Mississippi, Florida, Arkansas, and throughout Alabama. Many were dedicated to teaching agricultural skills.[19].[20] If they lacked the means or inclination to create schools, alumni also spread their knowledge throughout the South through informal, neighborly instruction.

For proof that Booker T. Washington saw agriculture as a strategy of resistance, we need look no further than the Negro Farmers Conference, which he organized through Tuskegee. Four hundred farmers from the Black Belt and beyond attended the first conference in 1892. Conference attendees doubled to eight hundred in 1893; by 1898, over two thousand farmers traveled from all parts of the South to attend.[21] Those attending the conference discussed crop diversification, strategies to increase landownership among African Americans, and related agricultural issues.

In its first year, the conference adopted the Declaration of Colored People in the Black Belt. This document emphasized the importance of landownership and homeownership and the ability of African Americans to grow their own food. It proposed to expand the sparse network of schools for black children in the Black Belt and, contrary to the norm of the school year being condensed for black children in order to allow them to work the farm during the typical school season, the Declaration initiated efforts to extend the school year into the growing season. By providing farmers the opportunity to discuss strategies of pooling together their meager resources to purchase land and seeds and to share labor, this conference laid essential groundwork for the establishment of black agricultural cooperatives. A local paper wrote that "every community" should have a black farmer's conference as a space to collectively address issues of farming as a means to self-sufficiency, reflecting a vision of the scope of the eventual cooperative movement.[22]

Farmers reported the progress from their communities annually at the conference. They posed questions directly to Washington and other distinguished members of Tuskegee's faculty. For example, at the 1904 meeting, a local farmer named Green Weldon of Butler County, Alabama, reported that five black people in his township had purchased land, two families had built houses, and four had added rooms to their homes. The town's African Americans had acquired a school, and few carried debt. Weldon also reported on his own success. He had owned nothing at the time of

Tuskegee Farmers Institute, c. 1910. George Washington Carver, far left top row. The Tuskegee University Archives, Tuskegee University.

the previous conference but now had a five-room home on 350 acres with "glass lights all the way round."[23] He and his wife, whose $150 annual earnings in egg money he acknowledged with pride, had thirteen children. He had been primarily responsible for building the community's schoolhouse. Reports like these document the importance of farming as a basis for self-reliance and self-sufficiency as well as the relationship between Tuskegee, Booker T. Washington, and the farmers themselves.

MEETING THE FARMERS IN THE FIELD:
BLACK COOPERATIVE EXTENSION

The creation of the Cooperative Farm Demonstration by the U.S. Department of Agriculture (USDA) in 1902 led to another significant contribution by Washington to black farmers' lives and future.

A ravenous boll weevil infestation, concentrated in Texas and Louisiana, was threatening the cotton crop and, therefore, the entire southern economy. The USDA's demonstration agents were charged, by Seaman Knapp, special agent of Farmers' Co-operative Demonstration Work and considered the founder of agricultural education and extension,[24] with providing resources to resolve the threat and to address other weaknesses in the farming sector. They went to rural areas of the country to offer assistance to farmers through education on progressive farming methods, including new technology, novel crop varieties, and the importance of crop diversification to avoid soil nutrient depletion. In the first three years, none of these agents were black, and white agents refused to talk to black farmers, whether they were sharecroppers, tenant farmers, or landowners. This was despite the fact that African American farm workers actually outnumbered whites in the South, yet the agents operated as if they could save the South while ignoring its majority.[25]

After Washington referred Thomas Moore Campbell, a Tuskegee alumnus, to the USDA, he became the first African American field agent in 1905.[26] Campbell was initially charged with meeting the needs of black farmers in Macon County, where Tuskegee is located. Ultimately he directed a team of farm agents with the responsibility for serving black farmers and their families throughout the South, which meant he served far more people than any white demonstration agents did.[27] Tuskegee became the district headquarters and offered space to the agents, an unusual role for a college to play for the USDA.[28]

Funded by the USDA, the Negro Cooperative Farm Demonstration Service, like its white counterpart, sent male farm agents and female home demonstration agents into the field to offer technical assistance through farm and home demonstrations. Farm demonstration agents offered men workshops and classes on new crop varieties; land, soil, and water conservation; marketing; and crop rotation. Women received home demonstration training in family health and nutrition, sewing, household management, and child-rearing.[29] Black extension agents met black farmers where they were—in the fields, after church services, outside of school buildings, and on plantations. They offered crash courses and demonstrations. The work of the farm and home demonstration agents responded not only to the needs of the community for more effective agricultural techniques but also to inadequate health care services for rural black families. The number of agents grew rapidly, from one in 1906 to 846 in 1950 with a reported benefit to 435,000 rural, black families[30]

Black extension agents often operated in politically precarious positions and were not always welcomed in communities. Many African American farmers, who had little reason to trust government agents, received them with suspicion. At the same time, white landowners saw them as improving the lives of their workers by increasing their self-reliance and autonomy, and therefore as a threat. Many localities required black agents to receive the permission of local white landowners and politicians before they could offer their demonstrations and agriculture-related lessons.[31]

WASHINGTON'S IMPACT AND INFLUENCE

Washington's direct role in helping black farmers was more straightforward. Mary Simpson, who attended one of Tuskegee's Farmers Conferences, credited Washington with her accomplishments: "I always tried to follow the advice of Booker T. Washington. I would never take up all my credit at the store. I would take eggs, chickens and other things to town to sell for what I needed in exchange. Now I sell cream. I have Barred Rock chickens and a good grade of hogs. I plant cover crops. All my hilly lands are terraced and my tenant houses are ceiled. I have two tenants, one on each place."[32]

Historian Allen W. Jones calculates that Washington's contributions benefited more than a million black southern farmers.[33] Tuskegee was the first large-scale program of any kind in the United States to support the agricultural version of the American Dream for those who were emancipated and their descendants. It was a fully functioning institution half a century before the lynching of Emmett Till sparked outrage, more than a decade before Rosa Parks was born in Tuskegee,[34] and four years after *Plessy v. Ferguson* affirmed the standard of separate but equal. The college and its founder thus deserve some measure of credit for the fact that the value of black-owned land in the South increased more than sevenfold by 1920. The multiple institutions that Washington established to serve African Americans, as well as the many he inspired and supported, continue to support black farmers.[35] Today, as African Americans turn to their ancestral agricultural roots, use food production as a strategy of rebuilding cities and creating alternative food systems for sustainable, healthy communities, reckoning with and even reclaiming Washington's legacy is critical. It can be done without ignoring those public statements he made that reflected the profoundly racist system in which he functioned.

Washington had a real impact on black farmers and their ability to achieve self-sufficiency and self-reliance. He articulated the value of his contribution himself when he wrote, "If a negro farmer in the cotton belt can feed himself and his family he is bound to become a respectable member of society; for in order to do it, he must own and not rent his house and his mules."[36]

George Washington Carver and Scientific Agriculture as Self-Sufficiency

Washington's goal in creating Tuskegee would have had a profound impact in its own right, but his decision to bring George Washington Carver onto the faculty in 1896 magnified that impact enormously.[37] Carver was a brilliant scholar with advanced degrees in botany who had written a long list of publications on plant breeding and grafting. Seeking to specialize the course offerings and scholarship in ways that would meet the needs of black farmers and their families, Washington considered Carver the only logical choice. As Carver's biographer points out, he was the "only black man in the country who had graduate training in 'scientific agriculture.'"[38] Carver was committed to land conservation, plant breeding, the study of plant disease and bacteriology, medicinal herbs, dietary recommendations, and what was known at the time as chemurgy—that is, finding uses for agricultural products in manufacturing.[39] His purpose was to provide the intellectual means by which sharecroppers or tenant farmers could make enough profit to purchase their land, feed their families, and achieve economic autonomy using agriculture as a strategy of self-sufficiency and sustainability. Carver added to Washington's project at Tuskegee the capacity to conduct independent scientific research in service of black farmers and to disseminate that scholarship to promote their economic independence and self-sufficiency.

Interest in Carver's work has surged recently, as evidenced by new scholarship and biographies.[40] Yet this scholarship tends to focus on his career as a scientist, including his contributions to botany and agriculture, without considering the larger purposes his science served. Most writings about his life are biographies written for young people that describe Carver as an almost mythological figure who, born into slavery, overcame adversity to pursue a scientific career. These books emphasize his research and inventions with peanuts and soybeans over his ideas about race, the economic self-sufficiency of African American farmers, his determination to provide farmers with a means of survival on the land, or his work as an environmental scientist whose scholarship contributed greatly to the field of sustainable agriculture.[41] The dearth of scholarly materials that connect Carver's work to the current demand for organic and locally grown foods represents an erasure of his commitment to scientific agriculture as a strategy of food and feed security. I seek to recover Carver's ecological framework for understanding the relationship of humanity to soil and to connect his work to the current resurgence of urban agriculture. This resurgence—whether its participants know it or not—has direct roots in Carver's work.

Like Washington, Carver was born into slavery.[42] His father was killed in an accident before his birth. As an infant, he was kidnapped with his mother in a plantation raid. His mother, Mary, was sold in Arkansas, and George never saw or heard from her again. The plantation owner, Moses Carver, sent a Union scout to recover the young George for $300 and traded his prized horse, in exchange for him. Carver was then raised in the household of his enslavers. Several childhood illnesses and maladies left him frail and small in stature. He writes that in his early years, "my body was feeble and it was a constant warfare between life and death to see who would gain mastery."[43] Considered too small and fragile for labor-intensive outdoor farm work, Carver was set to work at indoor chores that included cooking, cleaning, sewing, embroidery, and laundry. As a child, he was fascinated with flora and fauna, and he kept a small, hidden garden that he populated with transplants. He kept the plot out of sight because gardening was not considered an appropriate activity for boys.[44]

After leaving the Carver plantation on his own at the age of eleven, Carver traveled to Neosho to attend a school for African Americans.[45] In search of a more challenging educational experience, he then traveled from Missouri to Kansas to Iowa, where he enrolled in Simpson College and then the State Agricultural College at Ames (which later became Iowa State University). Majoring in botany at the state college, he was able to study the plants that had been his lifelong love. During his studies, he learned to approach growing plants in a scientific way. He specialized in techniques of cross-fertilization and grafting. Carver also learned how to identify and treat plant diseases under the direct instruction of the well-respected mycologist L. H. Pammel, with whom he published experimental findings in numerous journal articles.[46] Carver completed his bachelor's and master's degrees at Iowa. His bachelor's thesis, titled "Plants as Modified by Man," was an analysis of his experiments on grafting and crossbreeding. In his graduate program, Carver studied plant pathology and refined his ability to identify and treat plant diseases.[47] Carver was the first African American student at Iowa Agricultural College and the first black faculty member.

By the time his studies at Iowa ended, Carver had won national recognition for his scholarship. In 1896, Booker T. Washington offered Carver a job. His offer letter described Tuskegee thus: "Tuskegee Institute seeks to provide education—a means for survival to those who attend. Our students are poor, often starving. They travel miles of torn roads, across years of poverty. We teach them to read and write, but words cannot fill stomachs. They need to learn how to plant and harvest crops."[48] At the same time, Washington recognized that Carver's leaving his position on the faculty at Iowa

State would entail some sacrifice. He wrote, "I cannot offer you money, position or fame. The first two you have. The last, from the place you now occupy, you will no doubt achieve. These things I now ask you to give up. I offer you in their place—work—hard, hard work—the challenge of bringing people from degradation, poverty and waste to full manhood."[49]

Carver wasted no time in accepting Washington's offer. He appears to have recognized in Tuskegee the opportunity to do his life's work. His letter of acceptance notes, "It had always been the one great ideal of my life to be of the greatest good to the greatest number of 'my people' possible . . . [and I believe] this line of education is the key to unlock the golden door of freedom to our people."[50]

THE POOR PEOPLE'S SCIENTIST

Carver was appointed director of the Tuskegee Agricultural Experiment Station in 1897. In this capacity, he developed the School of Agriculture and ran the experiment station's ten-acre farm.[51] He also assumed primary responsibility for a number of outreach activities to farmers in the Black Belt.[52] In moving from an entirely white environment and community in Iowa to the predominantly black social setting in Alabama, he wanted to ensure that his work was beneficial for those he came to assist. Carver articulated his understanding of the importance of the moment for the study of agriculture, especially after the end of the institution of slavery, and suggested the kind of education that Tuskegee could offer in understanding the importance of nature to those with very little, "At no period of the world's history have the demands upon agriculture been so exacting than they are now . . . Let farmers' institutes be organized, and all the methods of nature study be brought down to the every-day life and language of the masses. Let us become familiar with the commonest thing about us."[53]

Carver's approach to science was premised on meeting the needs of those who needed it most. In keeping with Tuskegee's mission, he sought to ameliorate the health, economic, and environmental conditions of farmers in the Alabama Black Belt. He encouraged the Agricultural Experiment Station's open door policy—the practice of encouraging farmers to mail in or deliver plants and soil samples with questions they needed answered. He understood that answering these questions was important to putting money in the sharecroppers' pockets or food on their tables.

In addition to theoretically derived research questions that his contemporary academics formulated, Carver's research questions were rooted in the experiences of the tenant farmers and sharecroppers who sought to improve their lot in life. He was committed to producing knowledge that could be shared with them, as this statement demonstrates: "The primary idea in all of my work was to help the farmer and fill the poor man's empty dinner pail. . . . My idea is to help the 'man farthest down.' This is why I have made every process just as simple as I could to put it within his reach."[54]

Carver considered agricultural education to be a tool that black farmers could use to survive in racially hostile and economically oppressive environments. His work connected survivors of slavery and their descendants to new economic possibilities and therefore to freedom, promoting a sense of liberation among impoverished farmers in the rural South.

Carver believed that for agricultural science to be effective, it had to be connected to conditions on the ground. As he wrote in 1899, "The average southern farm has but little more to offer than about one-third of a cotton crop, selling at 2 and 8 cents per pound less than it cost to produce it, together with the proverbial mule, implements more or less primitive, and frequently a vast territory of barren and furrowed hillsides and wasted valleys."[55]

Carver was committed not just to conducting research in support of these farmers, but to producing and disseminating the results. To this end, the Agricultural Experiment Station at Tuskegee published its first bulletin based on Carver's research in 1898. The bulletins were published annually throughout his life (the final appeared after his death in 1943 but under his byline). The agricultural experiment staff—a farm manager, a horticulturist, a market gardener, a dairy head, someone responsible for raising livestock, and the librarian—worked with him to put it together. Each issue's ten to fifteen pages included articles that discussed a wide range of topics—from identifying wild foods that are edible, to what to grow, how to grow it, and how to process cultivated produce. They often included photographs and hand-drawn illustrations of experimental conditions. Articles addressed climate; soil fertility and remediation; the dangers of monocropping and the benefits of crop rotation and diversification; improving cash crops such as cotton and corn, investing in the production of food and feed crops such as sweet potatoes, cowpeas, tomatoes, and alfalfa; discussions of home beautification through the production and display of native ornamental plants; using plant-based materials for clays, stains, and paints; livestock care; and food preservation such as canning, pickling, and curing. The bulletin also contained discussions of foraging wild edibles, such as the wild plum and the acorn, which are available on the forest floor. Articles suggested medicinal uses for plants, both domestic and wild. They also addressed practical issues under titles like "How to Make and Save Money on the Farm" and "Twelve Ways to Meet the New Economic Conditions Here in the South."[56] Carver described the aims of these bulletins thusly:

> For eight years the Tuskegee station has made the subject of soil improvement a special study, emphasizing the subject of crop rotation, deep plowing, terracing, fertilizing, etc., keeping in mind the poor tenant farmer with a one-horse equipment; so therefore, every operation performed has been within his reach, the station having only one horse. . . . The chief aim was to keep every operation within reach of the poorest tenant farmer occupying the poorest possible soil worthy of consideration from an agricultural point of view and to further illustrate that the productive power of all such soils can be increased from year to year until the maximum of fertility is reached.[57]

The bulletins provided the level of detail a scientist seeking to assess and duplicate Carver's work would require but presented it in an accessible style. Carver strongly desired that his findings be accessible to farmers in the field. Under his advisement, F. H. Cardoza, in charge of horticulture, stated explicitly in the bulletin distributed in 1906, "This bulletin is written primarily for the colored farmers of Macon County and the state generally, and is meant to be not technical, but in the simple language for the average farmers to understand and put into practice."[58] Ten years after the first

Pig inoculation, Knapp Agricultural Truck. The Tuskegee University Archives, Tuskegee University.

bulletin, Carver stated that demand for access to previously published bulletins had exhausted a supply of 1,500 and that they would be reprinted.[59]

For farmers who could not read or did not receive the institute's bulletin, Carver worked with Tuskegee to develop a "moveable school."[60] The moveable school provided a more hands-on approach to disseminating scholarship. It began with Carver making weekend trips to rural communities to give talks and agricultural demonstrations.[61] Upon seeing the importance of these ventures, Washington requested that Carver, an avid technical artist, draw up a plan for a vehicle to be used for traveling through the rural areas—especially to schools, churches, and plantations—and offering demonstrations.

In all of his efforts, Carver recognized the limitations farmers faced. As he wrote in the bulletin, knowing that poor tenant farmers

Jesup Agricultural Wagon. The Tuskegee University Archives, Tuskegee University.

used "one-horse equipment," he described techniques that would accommodate these limitations.[62] Given the economic and structural conditions that many black farmers faced in this exploitative and oppressive system of sharecropping and tenant farming, Carver deplored their need to use outdated equipment and recognized that he could only be of help by respecting this limitation.

A HOLISTIC APPROACH TO AGRICULTURE: EXPERIMENTS AND INVENTIONS AT THE AGRICULTURAL EXPERIMENT STATION

Carver's scholarship consists of thousands of pages written over four decades. He wrote about scientific agriculture, which is the analysis and application of soil and plant sciences to land management, conservation, and crop production.[63] He believed that "the highest attainments in agriculture can be reached only when we clearly understand the mutual relationship between the animal, mineral, and vegetable kingdoms, and how utterly impossible it is for one to exist in a highly organized state without the other."[64]

While many agricultural historians and current practitioners and proponents of the local food movement consider J. I. Rodale—who wrote a highly influential book on organic agriculture in the 1940s—to be the father of sustainable agriculture, Rodale's work depended on Carver's. Through extensive agricultural experiments that included best growing practices and plant grafting and breeding, Carver provided evidence of the value of composting, crop rotation, and diversification—three basic tenets of organic farming. Carver was committed to identifying and overcoming the impediments to successful, sustainable agriculture. He was what today would be called a permaculturist, one who believes in the value of developing "Consciously designed landscapes which mimic the patterns and relationships found in nature, while yielding an abundance of food, fibre and energy for provision of local food needs."[65] Carver's work used sustainable products from organic, natural sources.

Corn and cotton, the South's longstanding cash crops, had significantly depleted southern soils.[66] Sharecroppers planted every inch of available land in the hopes of raising enough cash crops, such as tobacco and cotton, to pay for their use of the land. This often left little, if any, space on which to grow food for their families. The financial arrangement between landowners and sharecroppers left the farmers at a disadvantage, and they suffered from malnutrition, cycles of debt, and an inability to resist the crush of a deeply racist system. Sharecroppers and tenant farmers were already at a deficit in that they had access only to plots with the poorest soils. In addition, they had limited access to capital to improve the soil, purchase seeds, and hire additional labor. If the land produced at all, the farmers who had the weakest soil had the fewest financial resources to improve it and, given the economically exploitative sharecropping system, were left with the highest amount of debt, owing the landowners after an unproductive season.[67]

In the late 1880s, most of Alabama's largest farmers, heeding the advice of contemporary agriculturists, began to use commercial fertilizers. In contrast, with the needs of poor farmers in mind, Carver advocated cover crops—including legumes such as peanuts, cowpeas, and velvet beans—that could be used as food for humans and livestock but that also provided the soil with restorative nutrients. He suggested converting materials that were easily accessible, organic, and available on every almost every farm, such as food scraps and leaves, to compost. He studied the benefits of barnyard fertilizer—animal waste combined with compost.[68]

Carver's research led him to believe that composting was a key element of agricultural productivity. Many of his studies sought to identify the breakdown rates of various plant-based products that were easily accessible to farmers, thus allowing them to turn waste into nutrient-rich soil. Tuskegee's bulletins disseminated these findings throughout the region, providing details of the experiments—which Carver illustrated himself—and step-by-step instructions. In an era when few appreciated its significance, Carver waxed eloquent about composting: "[It] has increased the water-holding power of the soil to such an extent that a large number of the ragged, weedy and unsightly strips designated as terraces have been plowed out altogether, thus adding about one acre to the actual amount of land upon which crops are grown. Besides greatly improving the appearance of the field, it brought to the surface much latent fertility that had sunken below the depth to which the roots could penetrate by reason of the hard soil so near the surface."[69]

Carver also demonstrated the efficacy of "barnyard fertilizer" to improve soils. This resource was easily available to those raising livestock: "It is easy to see that our farm animals are great fertilizer factories, turning out the cheapest and best-known product for the permanent building up of the soil. In addition to this farm yard manure there are also many thousands of tons of the finest fertilizers going to waste all over the South in the form of decaying leaves of the forest and the rich sediment of the swamp known as 'muck.'"[70]

In an article that appeared in the 1936 bulletin, Carver described the importance of crop rotation as a strategy to rebuild soil to "virgin fertility"[71]: "Every progressive farmer recognizes that certain crops exhaust or make his soil poorer, and certain others build it up or make it richer. He is also aware that a better crop follows a pod-bearing one such as peas, beans, clover, vetches, peanuts, etc. Therefore they are absolutely indispensible in a wise crop rotation and in the rational feeding of both man and beast."[72]

In addition to his experiments with improving the soil, Carver sought to expand the range of crops and products that poor farmers used. The sweet potato was a particularly important crop for Carver. He identified both the soil-restorative benefits of growing the sweet potato and its health and nutritional value for humans and animals alike. Surprised that more farmers did not depend upon it for their own financial and health, he suggested as much: "The Colored farmers of Macon County alone ought to produce annually 1,000,000 bushels of sweet potatoes in addition to their cotton crops. A sweet potato is something that can always be used. It can be used to feed cows, pigs and chickens. Aside from this, there is always sale for sweet potatoes. . . . Let us all unite in making Macon County the banner sweet-potato-producing county throughout the entire south."[73] Carver was similarly smitten with the cowpea. Because of its marketability, he called it the "mortgage-lifter": "The cowpea is rightfully looked upon, by many, as the poor man's bank or mortgage-lifter. I think I am safe in the assertion that there is no crop grown in the South which possesses so many good qualities and is so easily grown as the cow pea. It is a matter of much regret that every colored farmer in Macon County does not plant at least three acres in peas."[74]

In addition, Carver promoted the daily consumption of fruit and vegetables to improve health as a strategy of self-sufficiency: "Fresh fruits and vegetables have a medicinal value, and when wisely prepared and eaten every day will go a long way towards keeping us strong, vigorous, happy, and healthy, which means greater efficiency and the prolonging of our lives. . . . If you carry out these suggestions you will be surprised how much healthier, happier, and how much more work you can do; and how quickly you will become self-supporting."[75] As a way to increase interest and acceptance, Carver even offered recipes for the crops he recommended: tomatoes, cowpeas, sweet potatoes, peanuts, and others.

Carver also tested foraged foods found in the woods for consumption by people and livestock. He created hundreds of plant-based products such as clays, paints, ink, wood fillers, cosmetics, laundry soap, and home remedies for a variety of medical conditions.[76] In a handbook titled *Help for the Hard Times,* Carver offered a calendar for farmers that included not only best practices with regard to when to plant, water, harvest, and weed, but emphasized how farmers could make money with these various value-added products made from plants during the off-season.

One measure of the respect Carver's inventions gained in their day is that Henry Ford asked him to assist with the development of peanuts and soybeans to create fuel, paint, and plastics for the burgeoning automobile industry.[77] Thomas Edison also offered Carver a six-figure salary to move to New Jersey to work in his labs. In a demonstration of his dedication to his work with black farmers, Carver refused, preferring to stay at Tuskegee.[78]

W. E. B. Du Bois and Prefigurative Politics

I propose as the next step which the American Negro can give to the world a new and unique gift. We have tried song and laughter and with rare good humor a bit condescending the world has received it; we have given the world work, hard, backbreaking labor and the world has let black John Henry die breaking his heart to beat the machine.

It is now our business to give the world an example of intelligent cooperation so that when the new industrial commonwealth comes we can go into it as an experienced people and not again be left on the outside as mere beggars. . . . If leading the way as intelligent cooperating consumers, we rid ourselves of the ideas of a price system and become pioneer servants of the common good, we can enter the new city as men and not mules.[79]

As intellectual precursors of collective agency and community resilience (CACR), Washington and Carver provide the institutional foundation and scientific knowledge for food production as a strategy of resistance and black community development. Especially in the postslavery/Reconstruction era—a time of great uncertainty, economic impossibility, racial hostility, and strife—they offered a vision of agriculture as a strategy of freedom and liberation. However, the work of W. E. B. Du Bois comes closest to the theoretical framework proposed in this book. His contributions to the sociological study of race and inequality, black political participation, social movements, economic behavior, and specifically the development of cooperatives represent the necessary pieces for a liberatory agriculture.

Arguably, Du Bois is more popular today than Washington and/ or Carver—and not just among sociologists, who after a long (racist) period of sidelining his contributions now revere him as a founding father of the discipline. But compared to Washington and Carver, Du Bois's contributions to the study of black agrarian realities and his arguments about the economic significance of cooperatives to the black freedom struggle have not been extensively reported. Du Bois was convinced that cooperatives were the key way to obtain freedom.

Three recent texts evidence a resurgence of interest in Du Bois's scholarship. In *The Scholar Denied: W. E. B. Du Bois and the Birth of Modern Sociology,* Aldon Morris (2015) draws on primary and secondary sources to argue that sociologists erased Du Bois's legacy by failing to recognize his contributions to the influential Chicago School of ethnographic field research and to the discipline in general. In an attempt to correct this marginalization, Morris shows that Du Bois's scholarship, which demonstrated the way that race interacts with economic and political factors, preceded similar research by those typically held to be sociology's founding fathers and thus demonstrates that Du Bois was actually one of the earliest founders of modern scientific sociology. Morris explains Du Bois's intellectual contributions to the field, his insistence on placing race at the center of analysis, and the ways racism led to his marginalization and to the erasure of his intellectual contributions.

Building upon Morris's work, Jakubek and Wood (2018) offer a thorough analysis of Du Bois's research that emphasizes his contributions to the study of African American rural realities. They argue that Du Bois was the "first American sociologist to conduct empirical analyses of agrarian production and case studies of rural communities," including small and large farms in the American South.[80] They note that the U.S. Department of Labor commissioned Du Bois to conduct five rural studies that investigated the experiences of black tenant farmers, sharecroppers, and land workers. One study that documented the conditions of rural poverty and social inequality among black sharecroppers in Lowndes Country, Alabama, was destroyed and never published.[81] Jakubek and Wood argue that Du Bois produced emancipatory empirical work documenting the experiences of African Americans and paid particular attention to the rural African American experience. Citing Du Bois's work on black rural communities in the post-Reconstruction period, they call Du Bois the first rural sociologist. With emphasis on his emancipatory empiricism, Jakubek and Wood suggest that Du Bois originated the black intellectual tradition of social justice empirical research.[82]

In her book *Collective Courage: A History of African American Cooperative Economic Thought and Practice*, Jessica Gordon Nembhard, a professor of community justice and social economic development details the broad history of African American cooperativism in the United States and delves directly into Du Bois's contribution to the understanding of African American cooperatives.[83] Citing his research on the Co-operative League of America, Nembhard identifies Du Bois as the first scholar to study black cooperatives and argues that his scholarship on them recovers a "continuous and hidden history of economic defense and collective well-being."[84] She quotes Du Bois: "There exists today a chance for the Negroes to organize a cooperative state within their own group. By letting Negro farmers feed Negro artisans, and Negro technicians guide Negro home industries, and Negro thinkers plan this integration of cooperation, while Negro artists dramatize and beautify the struggle, economic independence can be achieved. To doubt that this is possible is to doubt the essential humanity and the quality of brains of the American Negro."[85]

All of these roles describe a system of moving any product from the point of production to consumption and capture Du Bois's contributions to the origins of the discipline of sociology, engaging in emancipatory methodology and the development of a theoretical framework that would posit cooperatives as a strategy of resistance for black communities in the face of racial hostility and oppression. Du Bois was a crucial intellectual precursor to a model of collective agency and community resilience as practiced in the agricultural cooperatives described in this book. This section will concentrate on Du Bois's scholarship and activism on black cooperative development. Throughout his voluminous life's work, he studied, theorized, and organized cooperatives and revealed their role in a path to freedom. The first manuscript to pay particular attention to black collective action and cooperative development was *Economic Co-operation among Negro-Americans*, which is a comprehensive study of African American cooperatives and collectives. Written in 1907, it provides crucial context for understanding the role of cooperatives. It pays specific attention to the implementation and importance of black cooperatives and collectives as a strategy toward liberation. The second piece for understanding his perspective on cooperatives is evident in *Dusk of Dawn: An Essay toward an Autobiography of a Race Concept.* In this essay, originally published in 1940 as a partial autobiography, Du Bois argues that successful cooperative development could ultimately lead the African American community from a state of segregation, where exploitation and oppression exist, to freedom. Du Bois not only wrote about cooperatives, but he also translated his ideas into practice. He created the Negro Cooperative Guild in 1918 to provide political education and to offer training and skills for African Americans who sought to create cooperative businesses.

STUDYING COOPERATIVES

Atlanta University and the Carnegie Institute contracted Du Bois to write a series of manuscripts on the state of black America.

The twelve studies Du Bois produced addressed the political, so-cial, economic, employment, and educational status of African Americans. The twelfth, *Economic Co-operation among Negro Americans*, describes the history and trajectory of the development of cooperative efforts as part of the political and economic strate-gies that were critical for survival and for efforts toward freedom from oppression and discrimination.

Economic Co-operation among Negro Americans is a compre-hensive review of previous scholarship and documentation of black collective behavior and cooperatives dating back to the nine-teenth century. The study illuminates the mobilization efforts of generations of African Americans, the ways they were funded, and how they operated. Du Bois demonstrates the long, rich history of African Americans' collective behavior and economic cooperative development through an extensive review of archival records and available organizational literature. He offers a diasporac analysis of these collectives, connecting American black collectives and co-operatives with counterparts in Africa and the West Indies and the new colonies. Focusing on the question, "How far is there and has there been among Negro Americans a conscious effort at mu-tual aid in earning a living?" he provides evidence that African Americans have long worked to pool resources and efforts for po-litical, economic, and social gain.[86] Du Bois details the many ways African Americans cooperated and also the reasons that many of their organizations failed. In spite of the sad conclusions, Du Bois's description of what was done in the name of freedom and libera-tion provides an inspiring model.

These early efforts in "mutual aid in earning a living" prefigured the development of cooperatives.[87] Du Bois describes how African American communities created the social institutions that com-munity building and development required through cooperative efforts. Beginning with the church as a social institution, Du Bois discusses its significance as a cornerstone in black community building, with its roots in traditional African religions. For him, black churches served as a critical pathway to political organ-izations that led the way to economic self-determination. In his account, both traditional African religions and the black church functioned as safe spaces, as places where people could talk about and exercise spiritual, religious, and economic cooperation. As he wrote, the black church was the site of organization for insurrections and the interracial efforts of the Underground Railroad. After emancipation, black churches maintained its organizational center. The pooling together of tithes and offerings functioned as a form of economic cooperation that paved the way to beneficial and burial societies and that provided services for those who suffered from extreme conditions of poverty, especially under the oppressive conditions of plantation agriculture. Du Bois draws a compelling connection from the church to literacy encouraged by Sunday school, to burial societies and black cemeteries, to illness and burial insurance, to black settlement towns, and ultimately to the nation's first black-owned banks.[88] These examples of sharing offer an early example of commons as praxis. When people had little or no money, they worked together to provide for the community.

THEORIZING COOPERATIVES

Du Bois's investigation into the history of cooperatives led to his increasing belief in them as the tool of the black community's future. In a speech given in 1907 to the Negro Cooperative League, Du Bois said, "We unwittingly stand at the crossroads—should we go the way of capitalism and try to become individually rich as capitalists, or should we go the way of cooperatives and economic cooperation where we and our whole community could be rich together?"[89]

Du Bois recognized that Jim Crow segregation made both of these paths difficult. But he also argued that segregation offered space for the black community to create cooperatives as a strategy to achieve freedom from social, political, and economic oppression. His position was clear: through separation comes the opportunity for unification, combined with a political education of alternatives, which he argued would lead to political and economic autonomy. As if to respond to the question of the possibility for success using cooperative efforts as a strategy to achieve freedom, Du Bois identified the black community's rich history of establishing and funding its own institutions. On this issue, Du Bois and Washington were closer than their well-publicized debate would lead us to believe. Both saw a map toward freedom based on skills that the black community already possessed. Not unlike Washington's belief in the role of workers, Du Bois had confidence that the black community had the skills to create the basis for their own liberation: "We not only build and finance Negro churches, but we furnish a considerable part of the funds for our segregated schools, we furnish most of our own professional services in medicine, pharmacy, dentistry and law. We furnish some part of our food and clothes, our home building and repairing and many retail services. We furnish books and newspapers; we furnish endless personal services like those of barbers, beauty shop keepers, hotels, restaurants."[90]

Even while arguing for the elimination of segregation, he proposed that the black community "take advantage of it by planting secure centers of Negro co-operative effort and particularly of economic power to make us spiritually free for initiative and creation in other and wider fields."[91] In addition to other benefits, he proposed that this power would "eventually [break] down all segregation based on color or curl of hair."[92]

In contrast to the deficit-based approach that is common among academics when addressing issues of the black community, Du Bois's analysis offered an asset-based approach that focused on community strengths and resources. Du Bois called for laborers, miners, and those in transportation to work in "productive industries designed to cater to Negro consumers."[93] He wrote: "Already Negroes can raise their own food, build their own homes, fashion their own clothes, mend their own shoes, do much of their repair work, and raise some raw materials like tobacco and cotton. A simple transfer of Negro workers, with only such additional skills as can easily be learned in a few months, would enable them to weave their own cloth, make their own shoes, slaughter their own meat, prepare furniture for their homes, install electrical appliances, make their own cigars and cigarettes."[94]

The idea of the talented tenth that was so prominent in Du Bois's other writing does not show up to the same degree in his work on black agriculture and black cooperatives, where his vision was far more inclusive and closer to Washington's. Black labor, including farm labor, was a critical starting point in the development of large-scale cooperatives because of workers' ability to transform raw materials into goods and services. The markup between the actual cost and the selling price of goods and services served as the basis for individual profit and, ultimately, the exploitation of black workers within capitalism. It is important to note that Du Bois believed that the world economy was facing the decline of capitalism.[95]

For Du Bois, cooperatives were the "realization of democracy in industry" and created a strategy for economic success as a way to navigate and ultimately resist segregation.[96] Black communities offered a committed consumer base whose needs a cooperative could fulfill. Pooling intellectual and economic resources would eliminate the need for competition, which often leads to an increase in expenses in advertising but would offer the added bonus of eliminating unemployment, risk, and the need for access to capital, all of which deeply complicated black business success.

Instead of centralizing the producer, Du Bois encouraged prioritizing the needs of the black consumer for those interested in building cooperatives that would offer a greater degree of social justice and economic equity for the community. These co-ops would offer a living wage and better working conditions by keeping the goods affordable. It is through distribution that black communities and their cooperatives are able to connect to others. Ultimately, it is the resource regeneration that cooperatives provide that creates the economic force that eliminates the oppression that is indicative of a resource extraction model. Du Bois posited that producers would have no choice but to "respond to the needs of Black consumers." He told black workers that by leveraging this power, "tomorrow we may work for ourselves, exchanging services, producing an increasing proportion of goods which we consume and being rewarded by a living wage and by work under civilized conditions."[97]

Du Bois's theorization of cooperatives is surprisingly similar to current descriptions of a sustainable food system: both argue the importance of moving from food production, to distribution, to consumption and other aspects of the productive process. Du Bois's addition was that this is a pathway to freedom: "Easily obtainable technique and capital would enable Negroes further to take over the whole of their retail distribution, to raise, cut, mine and manufacture a considerable proportion of the basic raw material, to man their own manufacturing plants, to process foods, to import necessary raw materials, to invent and build machines. Processes and monopolized natural resources they must continue to buy, but they could buy them on just as advantageous terms as their competitors if they bought in large quantities and paid cash, instead of enslaving themselves with white usury."[98] He extended this logic to other areas of life, such as health care and insurance. He argued that these could "become a cooperative service to equalize the incidence of misfortune equitably among members of the whole group without profit to anybody."[99]

Du Bois described the necessity for an educated populace as a pathway to success for these cooperatives, demonstrating prefigurative politics as a mechanism toward economic autonomy: "Consumers' cooperatives into wholesales and factories will intensify the demand for selected leaders and intelligent democratic control over them—for the discovery of ability to manage, of character, of absolute honesty, of inspiration push not toward power but toward efficiency, of expert knowledge in the technique of production and distribution and of scholarship in the past and present of economic development."[100]

BUILDING COOPERATIVES

We spoke last month of the great call for team work on the part of American Negroes and the pressing necessity of turning that team work toward helping us to earn a living. Today the way is open for co-operation among 12,000,000 people on a scale such as we have never dreamed. What we can do is shown in little things. Ten thousand of us march.[101]

Du Bois's work on cooperatives was more than important to his body of scholarship; it was central. Biographers have described this work as "one of the most important contributions of his life" in his own estimation.[102] Demonstrating the concept of praxis—that is, the application of both theory and practice—he sought to support a national umbrella organization for the development of black cooperatives. In October 1918, in his capacity as a founding member of the NAACP and the first editor of *The Crisis* magazine, the organization's official journal, Du Bois called a meeting of twelve African American men from seven states to begin what would be called the "Negro Cooperative Guild."[103] The purpose of the meeting was to engage in discussions on the importance of cooperatives, to "introduce individuals and groups to study consumers' cooperation," and to promote that cooperation among African Americans.[104]

Intended to build the national organization and to create space for collective action, the assembly shared best practices and considered how its members might pool resources. Du Bois believed that political education was critical to the development of black cooperatives. According to Nembhard, the guild was "a national study circle [created] to inspire Black cooperative business development around the country . . . [to promote] cooperative economics, democratic participation, and business development, with a focus on the education program."[105]

Drawing on his historical and theoretical work on cooperatives, Du Bois envisioned the guild as a financial powerhouse that would support collectives at the local level. His model called for beginning with basic needs such as food, clothing, and jobs, but ultimately providing the black community with economic power that served as the foundation of "democratic control over industry."[106] Once organized, these cooperatives would provide services for the black community such as education, health care (including hospitals and medicine), banking, insurance, and law, later expanding to wholesale and manufacturing establishments.[107] In a description of the guild meeting he wrote a year later, Du Bois stated, "Cooperation aims at something else besides the establishment of food and clothing stores. Its main object is organization among a people who are in sad lack of that particular thing. [The Guild] hopes to introduce insurance against unemployment, sickness, old age; to establish a system whereby loans can be made to deserving members without the onus of high interest rates. It aspires to help out in time[s] of strikes and lock-outs, to provide club houses, hospitals, recreation centres. . . . Co-operation established the spirit of brotherhood."[108] The connection Du Bois drew between cooperatives as a force for black community development and the goal of economic autonomy is illustrated by his description of what he called "garden cities," which he described as a key way of establishing "a progressively self-supporting economy that will weld the majority of our people into an impregnable, economic phalanx."[109]

One attendee, a Mr. Roddy, returned to Tennessee after the meeting and immediately began to organize a citizen's cooperative. In February 1919, the cooperative received a charter of incorporation after which it opened five stores and served 75,000 members throughout the state of Tennessee. As the ensuing article in *The Crisis* recounted, "It was made plain to the members that the purpose of such an organization was to secure and protect the interest of their members. They themselves were to control the distribution of necessities and all profits were to be divided among them. The basis of division of profits rested on the amount of shares owned by each member, however, and not on the amount of goods purchased, which is the better plan."[110]

Nembhard suggests that the examples of the Negro Cooperative Guild and the cooperative stores it led to in Tennessee was "how advocacy, public education, self-education can promote cooperative development in the Black community [and] how cooperatives in low-income communities can be made affordable (shares can be bought in installments), and how cooperative businesses can be improved."[111]

As a field of study, a theoretical framework, and a liberation strategy, Du Bois's scholarly contribution to the African American cooperative effort provides a critical addition to my argument about the centrality of agriculture for black community development. Not only does his historical work document the existence of collective action and cooperative development for black communities, but his theoretical framework explains the advantages they provide, and his political work encouraged the development of cooperatives. Du Bois's legacy for contemporary black farming movements is twofold.

First, agriculture must be understood as part of a larger system, a point that prefigured what later came to be called agricultural systems analysis, as seen in the work of Bill Friedland.[112] Du Bois was prescient in connecting the work of farmers as producers to the community as consumers using an interconnected system of distribution and in calling for the connection of black communities across geographical locations. Second, Du Bois insisted that for agriculture to be pursued as a liberatory strategy, it must be done collectively. Both of these points have tremendous implications for today's urban agriculture and food justice activists.

The Legacy of the Three Wise Men

Du Bois's work illustrates the components of CACR. Demonstrating prefigurative politics, his emphasis on utilizing segregated spaces where those who are oppressed may strategize for their freedom is clear, applicable to the present, and progressive. His insistence that black cooperatives adopt the Rochdale principles that encourage collective decision making provided a place for those who were disenfranchised from the right to vote to practice democracy. This was also consistent with his socialist sensibilities and his critique of capitalist institutions.

While his early work was focused largely on what he called the "talented tenth," where an average of ten percent of the African American community would be what he considered the leadership class, in his work on cooperatives, Du Bois developed strategies that were meaningful to the larger black community. Like the other cooperatives this book describes, the organizations Du Bois created provided an opportunity for black farmers to move collectively toward their own freedom. Du Bois's vision of the cooperative contributed to the development of a community's ability to build economic autonomy, as illustrated in the ways that he suggested meeting the food, health, legal, and educational needs of the black community by building upon what he calls the "partially segregated Negro economy," building these cooperatives based on producers and consumers is a way to provide the needs and to expand the resources. By definition, cooperatives enact commons as praxis as they provide frameworks for sharing resources for the collective good.

While Du Bois and Washington began from very different premises—Du Bois from a version of socialism and Washington from a firm belief in capitalism—both contributed foundations for a distinctively black agriculture. The work of both men demonstrated care for black farmers and the value of agricultural work as a form of independence and self-reliance. Combining aspects of the legacies of Du Bois with those of Washington and Carver provides grounding for understanding the complicated and rich history of African Americans' relationship to the land. The oppression of slavery, land tenancy, and sharecropping is but one part of the story. These three wise men laid the foundation for an important counternarrative. Along with the many farmers and practitioners who worked alongside them, they developed an important theory and practice of a distinctly African American agriculture that was nourished in autonomous institutional spaces but has gone on to inform agriculture more broadly. Booker T. Washington's emphasis on agriculture as institution building, George Washington Carver's scholarship on scientific agriculture, and W. E. B. Du Bois's vision of the collective yet liberatory potential of cooperatives with agriculture at their base offer a different way of conceptualizing the relationship of African Americans to land.

Together, the intellectual traditions of black agriculture provide a framework that emphasizes the connection between agriculture and freedom. This framework has value for urban farmers and gardeners today who are reconnecting with the soil as a strategy of self-determination and self-sufficiency. These black intellectual traditions paved the way for current conversations about sustainable, organic, and local food, as well as food security and food sovereignty. They challenge the idea that community agriculture is something new and capture the radical components of the collective and the cooperative strategies that communities use to rebuild themselves using food production and distribution as strategies.

There is one important gap in the works of these three men. Nowhere in their frameworks did they mention women's agricultural vision, labor, or strategies. Like the world around them, they ignored the contributions of women to a distinctively black agricultural tradition. The archives reveal women farming, attending the farmers conferences, and participating in the moveable school demonstrations, among other examples. Their knowledge and perspectives are not acknowledged in the work of these three scholars. It would be left to someone who was not a scholar but who was an organic intellectual to bring to the forefront an example of how agriculture can be used as a strategy of resistance, resilience, and community building.

PART II
Collective Agency and Community Resilience in Action

2

A Pig and a Garden

Fannie Lou Hamer's Freedom Farm Cooperative

Down where we are, food is used as a political weapon. But if you have a pig in your backyard, if you have some vegetables in your garden, you can feed yourself and your family, and nobody can push you around. If we have something like some pigs and some gardens and a few things like that, even if we have no jobs, we can eat and we can look after our families. —Fannie Lou Hamer

In order for any people or nation to survive, land is necessary. —Fannie Lou Hamer

Fannie Lou Hamer founded Freedom Farm Cooperative (FFC) in 1967 as an antipoverty strategy to meet the needs of impoverished residents of Ruleville, Mississippi, in Sunflower County. Freedom Farm was a community-based rural and economic development project. Its members were unemployed farmworkers who had been dispossessed of access to land and displaced by mechanization. This chapter will show how Hamer's work manifested the basic principles of CACR. It offers an analysis of the political philosophy that led Hamer to create Freedom Farm as an alternative to the second wave of northern migration—the departure from the rural South for northern cities and manufacturing work. Freedom Farm represented an opportunity to stay in the South, live off of the land, and create a healthy community based upon building an alternative food system as a cooperative and collective effort. It was in keeping with Hamer's perspective that if she had a pig and a garden, "she might be harassed and physically harmed but at least she would not starve to death."[1]

Born Fannie Lou Townsend in 1917, Hamer was the twentieth child of sharecroppers. She worked in the fields of the Marlowe Plantation in Ruleville, Mississippi, from the age of six.[2] She gained a sixth-grade education and stopped attending the seasonal school to work in the fields full-time by the age of thirteen.[3] Contemporaries recalled with some amazement that as a teenager she could pick two hundred to three hundred pounds of cotton per day, as much as many twice her age.[4] But she was struck with polio in young adulthood, which left her with a limp. She married Perry "Pap" Hamer and experienced involuntary sterilization when she underwent surgery to have a uterine tumor removed.[5] The State of Mississippi endorsed such acts of violence as a means to curtail the rates of African American births.[6] While she and Pap adopted three daughters over the course of their long marriage, she never forgave the state of Mississippi for her forced sterilization, referring to it caustically as a "Mississippi appendectomy."[7]

In 1962, Hamer attended a mass meeting sponsored by the Student Nonviolent Coordinating Committee (SNCC) in Ruleville and was among the first to volunteer as a field organizer to coordinate and organize the voter education and registration drives. Later that year, she led a group of African Americans to the state courthouse in Indianola, Mississippi, that applied for voter registration. The state claimed that the entire group had failed the "literacy" exam, a qualification Mississippi and other states used at the time to disenfranchise African Americans. Upon her return to Ruleville, after eighteen years of dedicated service as sharecropper, time- and record-keeper, cook, and domestic on the Marlowe Plantation, Hamer's boss demanded that she withdraw her application for voter registration or be fired. Her refusal not only led to her dismissal but also eviction for her and her husband, Pap, as they rented a shanty as part of their sharecropping-employment agreement.

About the firing, Hamer later commented, "They kicked me off the plantation, they set me free. It's the best thing that could happen. Now I can work for my people."[8] The costs continued to mount in 1963, when Hamer was arrested for registering to vote. In jail, a group of black inmates was forced by law enforcement officers to beat her. She suffered permanent kidney damage from the incident.[9] It was the first of many brutal attempts to curtail her activism by Mississippi law enforcement officers,[10] many of whom held memberships in organizations such as the Ku Klux Klan and the White Citizens' Council.

Hamer became known throughout the civil rights movement for her oratorical skills and for calming organizers and activists by singing spirituals during contentious moments. Hamer's nationally televised testimony before the Credentials Committee of the Democratic National Convention in 1964, demanding that the committee seat her and sixty-seven other African American and white representatives of the newly formed Mississippi Freedom Democratic Party, stunned the nation. Challenging the all-white delegates officially representing the Mississippi Democratic Party, she succinctly described the acts of terrorism to which she had been subjected. She concluded, "If the Freedom Democratic Party is not seated now, I question America. Is this America, the land of the free and the home of the brave, where we have to sleep with our telephones off of the hooks because our lives be threatened daily because we want to live as decent human beings, in America?"[11]

President Lyndon Johnson called an emergency televised press conference to divert the nation's attention from Hamer, but his efforts backfired. The video recording of Hamer's powerful testimony was replayed several times throughout the convention and formed part of the backdrop to the long and contentious process leading to the passage of the Voting Rights Act of 1965. Hamer continued her participation in electoral politics with runs for Congress in 1964 and 1965, and the Mississippi State Senate in 1971, each of which she lost.[12] In 1968, the Mississippi delegation sent Hamer as an official delegate to the Democratic National Convention.

Center for Activism: Sunflower County

Hamer presumably chose Sunflower County as the site of FFC because it was home, where she had connections and relationships of trust. There was also dire need there. If Mississippi sought to starve black residents into compliance with the racial hierarchy, it was succeeding in Sunflower County.[13] The county's rates of malnutrition, type 2 diabetes, hypertension, and other diet-related illnesses were among the highest in the nation. As elsewhere in the Jim Crow South, the state routinely denied impoverished African Americans public assistance and social services. Opportunities for employment were scant. Sunflower County's black population had the highest infant mortality rates in the country. When Tufts Medical School opened up a community clinic in 1967 in the neighboring county of Bolivar, a considerable percentage of the residents were diagnosed with conditions related to malnutrition. Most of the prescriptions written by physicians were for food. "There was as much food in the pharmacy as there was medicine," the Measure for Measure financial support proposal of 1978 reported.[14]

The 1960 U.S. Census reveals that Sunflower County's population of almost 46,000 was 67 percent African American, 32 percent white, and 0.4 percent other racial groups (Native American, Japanese, Filipino).[15] That year, the USDA bestowed a subsidy check of more than $167,000 on James Eastland, a wealthy Sunflower County planter and U.S. senator. *Time* magazine aptly called Eastland "the spiritual leader of segregationists" in 1967. The check was marked for investment in increased mechanization in agriculture, not to plant cotton.[16] It led to the unemployment and homelessness of black families whose heads of households were primarily employed as agricultural workers, sharecroppers, tenant farmers, and farm managers.

Mississippi has consistently ranked high among U.S. states in poverty rates. In 1960, the median income of black families in the county was $1,126 per year.[17] In 1965, Mississippi was ranked the "poorest state in the Nation."[18] Federal efforts to respond to extreme hunger and malnutrition included a visit from Senate representatives from the Subcommittee on Employment, Manpower, and Poverty headed by Joseph Clark of Pennsylvania. The tour also included Senator Robert F. Kennedy. Hamer was among the many local residents, politicians, businesspersons, educators, and activists with whom they spoke. After their visit, they demanded that the Department of Agriculture begin more food programs throughout the state. However, Mississippi congressman Jamie Whitten, the powerful chairman of the Agricultural Appropriations Subcommittee, demanded an end to any data collection that would evaluate the economic situation of those in the area. Whitten fought to ensure that U.S. farm policy would never have a means to recognize the effects of its programs on sharecroppers or other farm workers.[19]

The Second Great Migration was a response to such policies. Between 1940 and 1960, more than three million black people fled southern states.[20] Mechanization and oppression left many black families with little choice but to seek better living conditions, education, and employment opportunities in northern urban areas.[21] In 1960, over 60 percent of the African American population in Sunflower County was employed in agriculture, forestry, or fisheries. Seventy percent of the black male population was employed in the agricultural industry as farmers, farm managers, laborers, and foremen. Twenty-five percent were employed as craftsmen, and non-farm laborers, in manufacturing and other service industry occupations. The remaining 5 percent worked as managers or in positions of sales, private households, or were unreported. Forty-two percent of black women were employed as domestic workers or day laborers, and an additional 36 percent worked as farmers, farm laborers, and managers. Ninety percent of the county's black population had six or fewer years of education. Between 1950 and 1960, Sunflower County's population decreased by 20 percent as African Americans moved north to the urban areas in northern cities, known as the Rust Belt, such as Detroit, Milwaukee, Chicago, Pittsburgh and west to California, two areas courting them with promises of employment and liberation from the exploitative economic conditions of Mississippi. Between 1960 and 1970, the county's population declined an additional 20 percent.[22]

An Organic Intellectual

Hamer's understanding of the facts on the ground in Mississippi reveals her to have been an organic intellectual. Antonio Gramsci argued that every social class creates organic intellectuals who articulate and identify the collective's objectives. They develop strategies, tactics, and remedies for rebuilding and responding to the economically and politically oppressive obstacles that complicate the lived realities of those whom they represent: "Every social group . . . creates together with itself, organically, one or more strata of intellectuals which give it homogeneity and an awareness of its own function not only in the economic but also in the social and political fields. . . . He [sic] must be an organiser of masses of men; he must be an organiser of the 'confidence' of investors in his business, of the customers for his product."[23]

Booker T. Washington, George Washington Carver, and W. E. B. Du Bois all had formal educations, advanced degrees, and credentials. Because they were employed as educators and researchers, many would have considered them to be traditional intellectuals. Hamer's background as a sharecropper and domestic worker with a sixth-grade education fed—rather than impeded—the sophistication of her intellectual achievements.

Applying Gramsci's concept of an organic intellectual to Hamer highlights that her words and works articulated the struggles and issues faced by those who were racially and economically disenfranchised. In her work with SNCC as a major organizer of Freedom Summer, Hamer supervised voter education drives, articulated the struggles of the oppressed, and challenged those whose efforts maintained the status quo.[24] She called out the black middle class, such as church leaders and educators, identifying them as accessories to the crimes of oppression. She also galvanized resources to respond to the immediate concerns of poverty, including hunger, shelter, health care, and housing. Hamer envisioned a model in which the community could achieve self-sufficiency, even within the context of the racially contentious Jim Crow state of Mississippi. Freedom Farm represented a piece of her long-term strategy of self-sufficiency.

In an interview with the Wisconsin-based magazine *The Progressive* in 1968, Hamer articulated the struggles of displaced farmworkers and the elite's intentional use of starvation as a strategy of oppression. Her interviewer summarized what she told him: "Down in Mississippi they are killing Negroes of all ages, on the installment plan, through starvation. If you are a Negro and vote, if you persist in dreams of black power to win some measure of freedom in white controlled counties, you go hungry. . . . There is a way to fight back against this 'non-violent' weapon of white officialdom" In Hamer's words: "Where a couple of years ago white people were shooting at Negroes trying to register, now they say, "go ahead and register—then you'll starve."[25] Hamer's organic intellectualism— her experience of the condition of starvation as a political weapon— enabled her to identify this structural obstacle to collective progress for the African American citizenry. She understood that the exploitative economic relationships between landowner and farm worker and between homeowner as employer and domestic worker were a major impediment to the movement for the vote. In her work with SNCC and with the Mississippi Freedom Democratic Party, she connected the starvation of people in Sunflower County not only to the pressure to migrate but also to the pressure not to register to vote: "Nobody told us we have to move from Mississippi. Nobody tells us we're not wanted. But when you're starving you know."[26] In creating Freedom Farm as a means to develop a sustainable black community on the foundation of agriculture, Hamer illuminated the relationship between economic self-sufficiency and political power and translated the theory into action.

Hamer's strategy connected landownership with voting rights. A 1971 article notes, "Fannie Lou Hamer emphasizes that the leverage of owning land and the fact that land supports people have given those people a wedge into the political machine—rich, white, and racist—that has always run Mississippi."[27] In the same article, Hamer argued simply, "Land is the key. It's tied to voter registration."[28]

As a political organization by and for black people (although it was open to farmers of any race), Freedom Farm brought Hamer's insight to life. By pooling resources, the community was designed to become self-sufficient and therefore able to resist political, social, and economic disenfranchisement and the pressure to relocate to the North. The organization sought to realize Hamer's vision of economic participation as the path to political participation, based on her organic intellectual understanding of the means of

oppression of the people of Sunflower County. By providing housing, health care, employment, education, and access to healthy
food that the white power structure of rural Mississippi denied
them, Freedom Farm provided a sphere for the development of a
free mind, an opportunity to create new identities, and a new form
of collective political consciousness. It used the strategies of commons as praxis, prefigurative politics, and economic autonomy to
achieve collective agency and community resilience.

Freedom Farm as Resistance

In creating Freedom Farm, Hamer intended to concentrate on
three primary areas: (1) building affordable, clean, and safe housing; (2) creating an entrepreneurial clearinghouse—a small business incubator that would provide resources for new business
owners and retraining for those with limited educational skills
but with agricultural knowledge and manual labor experience;
and (3) developing an agricultural cooperative that would meet
the food and nutritional needs of the county's most vulnerable.[29]
Local and regional white politicians and businesspersons had
lobbied Washington successfully to deny federal funding and antipoverty resources to impoverished black tenant farmers and
farm workers. Denying these farmers and workers food, housing,
education, and health care was part of their larger project of re-
stricting the vote and maintaining the racial hierarchy. No less a
figure than singer and political activist Harry Belafonte described
Freedom Farm's response in a fund-raising letter in March 1967:
"Now, to give hundreds of landless poor people a chance at self-
help, economic self-sufficiency and political power, Mrs. Hamer
has organized a farm cooperative. Acreage of fertile soil is available to the cooperative at exceptionally low cost. A community of
free, independent people can be built if financial help is given at
this time."[30]

Several Harvard University student organizations also were involved in fund-raising efforts for Hamer and Freedom Farm in this
period, leading the *Harvard Crimson* to write in 1970, "Mrs. Hamer
said that [FFC's] goal was not only to provide a farm income for

landless families, but also to serve as a social and political organizing center for the blacks of the Mississippi Delta."[31]

Hamer believed that leadership of Freedom Farm should be black and local; she was also very clear that membership and its privileges would be open to anyone who needed the assistance that Freedom Farm offered. At various times, membership rolls included a few families who identified as white. Membership fees were minimal.[32] Even so, inability to pay did not exclude members; during the first year, only thirty families paid dues, but Hamer claimed that hundreds of families belonged in name and that countless others benefited from Freedom Farm.[33] As a document of the time reported, "Freedom Farm Corporation is owned and worked co-operatively by about 1,500 member families in Sunflower County. Founded by Mrs. Fannie Lou Hamer, nationally recognized civil rights leader, the co-op presently owns 692 acres."[34]

In the context of a white supremacist establishment that did not hesitate to prevent political mobilizing through violent means, the mere survival of black agricultural cooperatives was a feat of resistance. Hamer created Freedom Farm to improve the living conditions of those who were unemployed and homeless while creating opportunities for farmworkers by utilizing their agricultural skills. Under her model of activism, black farmers could stay on the land and build a sustainable community through their own labor, and thereby secure a means to political participation. Through Freedom Farm, she continued her efforts in organizing and educating southern, rural farm workers about electoral participation, registration, and mobilization. As part of Freedom Farm members' efforts to organize land workers, they also actively participated in a political education campaign to educate residents of Sunflower County, using flyers and pamphlets that informed residents about their right to participate in the political process by voting.

Farmers and land workers who fought against structural and economic inequities inherent in tenant farming and sharecropping, those who spoke out against land and/or labor conflicts, and those who participated in voter registration and education drives experienced repression from local white farmers, business owners, politicians, and members of law enforcement. Hamer's own firing following her participation in a political action was typical, as the National Council of Negro Women (NCNW) reported: "The black man who dares speak out or even exercise his constitutional rights usually finds himself and his family thrown out onto the road, and often deprived of the few possessions he did have. 'They wouldn't even let me back in my place to get my clothes or a picture of my mother. I just had to leave everything there,' said one woman who was evicted after she registered to vote, following the 1964 civil rights legislation."[35]

In other cases, farmers were run off the land by threats against their lives. Some left the South with their families and traveled, under dark of night, to northern cities such as Detroit, Chicago, and Gary, Indiana.[36] Others were arrested and/or murdered.[37] The relationship between members of law enforcement and white supremacy organizations made any encounter especially dangerous, even fatal, through extralegal and legal violence such as lynchings, police brutality, and police complicity with mob violence. The murders of civil rights activists Medgar Evers, James Earl Chaney, Andrew Goodman, and Michael Schwerner typified the white racist response to the intense desire for racial equity and justice in Mississippi. The organizing of African Americans who demanded the right to vote and to participate fully in the political process posed a significant threat to Jim Crow, and the establishment fought in its defense.

Not all means employed by the white establishment to maintain the oppression of blacks in the South were extralegal. Mississippi passed laws aimed at debilitating the African American community's capacity to galvanize and work cooperatively for better living and work conditions. These laws rendered illegal many of the measures SNCC, NAACP, and CORE had embraced, including economic boycotts, picketing, and demonstrations. White business leaders, politicians, and law enforcement personnel invoked the state's Secondary Boycott and Criminal Conspiracy in Restraint of Trade Statute.[38] The law journal of Howard University characterized the statute thusly: "This statute imposes civil and criminal liability on any two or more persons who combine to conspire to prevent another person or other persons from doing business with a merchant, who induce or encourage another person or other persons to cease doing business with a merchant in order to effectuate a reasonable grievance over which the merchant has no direct control or legal authority to correct."[39]

Given this context, alternative strategies of resistance, such as agricultural cooperatives, were necessary for the survival of the movement to sustain activists, to provide them with a measure of independence so they could avoid joining the migration or being economically cowered to survive, and to sustain another sphere of struggle. NCNW, a key funder of Freedom Farm, conducted an annual review of the organization in its early years. The 1968 review stated, "The important part is that the people themselves have a stake in it; they are not relying on hand-outs; they are enhancing their own dignity and freedom by learning that they can feed themselves through their own efforts."[40] In keeping with this vision, FFC informed its members about the importance of their vote, encouraged them to run for election, and invited them specifically to identify potential candidates for the county committee of the Agricultural Stabilization and Conservation Service (ASCS). The ASCS was a major force in determining how federal funds would be allocated to local community, agricultural, and other antipoverty projects in the region. These positions were especially important because the allocation of funds for agriculture was one of the ways that elites had denied funding for black farmers and their organizations.

The federal Department of Agriculture issued subsidies to white landowners, planters and plantation owners to allow their land to go fallow, in order to control the price and profitability of cotton as well as to induce investment in innovative agricultural technology.[41] The immediate impact was a dramatic reduction in the amount of farm labor needed. The resulting surplus of labor made it easy for white landowners to render activists unemployed and homeless.

Against these odds, FFC was a community offering respect and fair exchange for members' labor, a place where they could grow and provide healthy food, and where they could secure safe and affordable housing as well as quality education, health care, and employment opportunities. As an alternative to being dependent upon a white power structure, FFC had bold goals.

Farming and Economic Autonomy

In an effort to increase access to healthy food, FFC's members worked collaboratively in planting, maintaining, and harvesting the crops in the community gardens. In the community spaces, thirteen of the first forty acres were dedicated to subsistence crops and community gardening, where co-op members planted greens, kale, rape, turnips, corn, sweet potatoes, okra, tomatoes, string, and butter beans.[42] In 1972, these subsistence crops served more than 1,600 families.[43] At least 10 percent of the community garden harvest was donated to needy families whose members were unable to work the fields. Cooperative families shared the remainder, and if there was more than they needed, FFC shipped the surplus to feed needy families as far away as Chicago.[44] Thus, they fed the neighbors who had left them in the Great Migration.

In pursuit of its goals of self-sufficiency, FFC set aside 540 acres to be used for a catfish cooperative and for grazing land for cattle to support the members who lived on the remaining hundred acres.[45] Two years later, they planted three hundred acres in cotton, 209 acres in soybeans, eighty acres in wheat, and ten acres of cucumbers[46] The income from these cash crops were sold to pay the mortgage on the land. While they had contracts with Atkins Pickle Company and Heinz, according to the historical records, it is unclear the degree to which they were able to fulfill them.

In 1969, NCNW donated approximately fifty pigs to FFC, forty-five white Yorkshire pregnant gilts (females) and five male Brown Jersey boars (males).[47] The animals quickly became local celebrities, affectionately known as the "Sunflower Pigs," and they began what was to be called the "Bank of Pigs" or the "Oink-Oink Project."[48] As NCNW's annual review described it, "The plan was not to provide instant food by butchering the livestock, but to breed them, thus establishing a 'pig bank,' which would be self-sustaining and will provide 300–400 new piglets out of the first litters."[49]

Community women built fences and shelters for the pigs, and the community men did the pig ringing, a process that would prevent the pigs from ingesting the parasitic ringworm. In its first U.S.-based project, Heifer International provided expert assistance

Freedom Farm Cooperative pig bank. Photo by Franklynn Peterson.

in the care, maintenance, and husbandry of the pigs. After reaching full maturity in two years, these pigs were to be mated, slaughtered for meat, or sold for supplemental income.[50] Families kept sows (grown females) and took them to a breeding facility that housed the boars.

Upon delivery of a litter, which typically included nine to twenty piglets, families deposited two piglets in the pig bank.[51] By 1969, the pig bank had provided over a hundred families with pigs, each of which produced over 150 pounds of meat.[52] In its third year, the number grew to three hundred families.[53] By 1973, more than 865 families were beneficiaries of the pig bank,[54] which had produced thousands of pounds of meat and thousands of dollars in supplemental income for member families.

Support for Housing

Hamer identified housing as another important cornerstone to community development. The condition of available housing in Sunflower County was deplorable. As the *Harvard Crimson* described it, "More than 95 percent of the county's blacks live in houses officially classified as 'dilapidated and deteriorating.'"[55] Additionally, 75 percent of homes in Sunflower County lacked running water, and 90 percent lacked indoor plumbing.[56] In 1969, more than a hundred families were evicted from shacks and tent homes where they resided on white plantations.[57] FFC helped

Freedom Farm Cooperative housing development, Ruleville, Mississippi. Photo by Franklynn Peterson.

members find housing and obtain mortgages and provided financial support to ensure that members stayed in their homes. Hamer articulated the importance of this project thusly: "The state wants us out and the government considers us surplus. We must buy land immediately or our people will die forgotten."[58]

In 1971, FFC put down a deposit of $84,000 on 640 acres of land east of Drew, Mississippi, to build additional housing. They developed the Delta Housing Development Corporation, with Hamer serving on the board of directors. In 1972, the U.S. Farmers Home Administration (FmHA) provided funding for eighty new "self-help houses," and construction began.[59] These new homes were wired for electricity and had running water and indoor toilets.[60] The FmHA released $800,000 in mortgage funds under its interest credit program, which enabled FFC members to take possession of the properties.[61]

At a speaking engagement, Hamer spoke about the program to provide affordable, adequate housing in the Jim Crow South: "The one kind of remark which really means the most to me is one that I hear frequently outside on really cold mornings. You'll see two men walking out their front doors. One will kind of stop, look around and say, 'Phew I didn't realize how cold it was outside!' Every place they ever lived in before, it was always just as cold inside as it was outside."[62]

FFC eventually went beyond renegotiating purchase agreements of homes to allow members to maintain their residences and assisting with the completion of the paperwork necessary to obtain new mortgages. In 1969 and 1970, FFC began to provide housing to members. The organization purchased ninety-two new housing lots, and seventy-three families received housing.[63]

Education

White planters had little incentive to support their laborers' children's education. Providing a quality education threatened the power and privilege they wielded in their economically exploitative relationship with their tenants and laborers. Classroom instruction usually occurred between December and April after the cotton had been picked and ginned and before the new planting season began. Schools in Mississippi had refused to desegregate after the *Brown vs. Board of Education* decision in 1954, and for the children of black tenant farmers and sharecroppers especially, the state invested little in its schools. Educators were often expected to teach classes for which they were unqualified. They worked under inferior conditions that included substandard facilities, overcrowded classrooms with several grades in a one-room schoolhouse, and old, often racially offensive books and reading materials. Children whose parents were unable to afford weather-appropriate clothing and shoes during the colder months were unable to attend even the seasonal schools.

The implementation of Head Start began to address these issues.[64] Freedom Farm Cooperative was selected as a site for one of the region's first Head Start programs, which served as an anchor of community-based development and as a marker of FFC's success. Hundreds of participating families received health and dental care, early educational experiences, and supplemental nutrition. Millions of dollars in federal funds from the Office of Equal

Opportunity were sent to community-based black organizations, including FFC, under the organizational banner of the Child Development Group of Mississippi. At one point, leaders of Head Start claimed to employ over one hundred workers and serve six hundred preschool children.[65] It had become a major employer for the county. The program served the young people of Sunflower County for several years before white-led protest over the black leadership of Head Start led to the withdrawal of millions of federal dollars dedicated to the program; nevertheless, most of the facilities found community sources of support to sustain them.

In addition to Head Start, FFC provided a number of types of vocational education. The work of building FFC's homes involved approximately twenty men, former farm workers, who were enrolled in the Housing Training program, which taught construction and home building; these men also assisted with building the community center that housed the FFC offices. The program was just one facet of FFC's education, employment, and skills retraining program. In addition to the Housing Training program, vocational educational learning opportunities included life skills such as food preservation, sewing, and childcare.

Employment

Freedom Farm was a major employer for Sunflower County. It provided full- and part-time jobs for over forty residents. Those jobs included secretary, bookkeeper, farm manager, and farm laborer positions for agricultural projects such as the community garden and the cash crops of cotton, soybeans, and tobacco.[66] FFC also employed summer youth workers who conducted community-needs assessments by fanning out throughout the county to survey residents whose identification of priorities FFC could use to recalibrate its programs.

FFC also developed two sewing cooperatives where members made clothes, and one clothing cooperative that recycled gently used clothing. Members made suede and leather handbags, quilts, African-style clothing, and hats.[67] FFC sold these wares through a storefront in Madison, Wisconsin, with 90 percent of the proceeds

Members of Freedom Farm Cooperative at the sewing cooperative. Photo by Franklynn Peterson.

going to pay the workers.[68] FFC paid all of its employees ten dollars per day, often supplementing the salary with housing, food, and services. One of the cooperatives even had an on-site day care center for the children of its workers.

Disaster and Poverty Relief

Historically in Mississippi, after the harvesting season—when cotton had been picked, ginned, packed, and sold—farm families were no longer working on the plantations, and many had no source of income. Some might do daywork in white families' houses as domestics or other service occupations. With meager finances for food and other incidentals, even when housing was provided as part of their employment package, many families needed support to survive the winter.

In order to respond to this seasonal scarcity, FFC held fund-raising drives for clothing, food, kitchen supplies, and school supplies such as books, paper, and writing utensils. In the absence of a secure location or community center, Hamer's personal residence often served as a distribution center for these goods.[69]

In 1969, with a generous donation from the NCNW, FFC developed a tool bank as another way to respond to seasonal poverty. Member families could borrow tools for specific projects that would provide self-employment income during the off-season. They could share the labor on projects if they needed support and help from others.

In times of disaster, FFC provided social services to adjoining counties as well as in Sunflower County, offering assistance such as temporary housing for victims of floods, tornados, and other emergencies. When a tornado struck, the organization provided support to more than three hundred people through its relief measures and through Delta Housing Development Corporation. They provided clothing assistance to some eighty families and aided others in paying overdue utility bills.[70] In 1972, FFC established a food stamp fund and provided financial assistance to twenty-five families to purchase food stamps.[71] It provided an additional fifty-seven families with support in applying for federal (public) assistance.[72] FFC also facilitated the Send-a-Box program, cosponsored with NCNW, to respond to the immediate food needs of residents in the Mississippi Delta. It was able to assemble approximately ninety food boxes for the relief of FFC members. FFC also instituted a family mobile health program.[73]

Fund-raising for FFC

Through her nationwide fund-raising efforts, Hamer brought international attention and resources to the extreme living conditions of those in the Mississippi Black Belt. FFC's members were extremely poor; self-sufficiency and self-sustenance could not be realized immediately. As she transitioned from her work on voter education and registration in the 1950s and into the 1970s, Hamer used the international reputation and attention her earlier political work had brought when she traveled to publicize the struggle of dispossessed land workers in Mississippi and to secure funding for FFC. The proceeds from her national and international speaking engagements provided some income for the organization.

Because of her reputation as a political organizer, Hamer was able to enlist the support of many well-known public figures, such as Harry Belafonte, who stated in a fund-raising letter, "A community of free, independent people can be built if financial help is given at this time. . . . Contributions of $10, $100, $1000 will start a pioneer development, giving a new life to Americans whose living standard is as low as that of the peasants of the underdeveloped world."[74]

As previous sections have demonstrated, the National Council of Negro Women was one of the primary organizations providing technical assistance and financial support. NCNW's historical records list Hamer as a county representative of the organization. The organization's annual reports on FFC achieved the buy-in of its membership, documenting the conditions under which Hamer and FFC acted and enabling FFC to purchase seeds for the community garden and undertake other projects. The subsistence crops FFC grew from these seeds yielded thousands of pounds of produce that FFC harvested to feed hundreds of families. NCNW's annual reports also effectively brought federal attention to the situation of those in the region.

Though the reasons are unclear from the historical record, NCNW withdrew its support from FFC in 1970. Hamer was able to replace the lost funding with support from Measure for Measure, a civil rights organization based in Madison, Wisconsin. Itself a collective—membership consisted of academics and progressive clergy—Measure for Measure donated tens of thousands of dollars, supplies for schools, clothing, and crucial and expensive materials, such as sewing machines for the sewing cooperative. The organization held fund-raising events in support of FFC as well as agricultural cooperatives in North Bolivar County (the subject of chapter 4), and in Mound Bayou, Mississippi. Measure for Measure held a walk against hunger in 1969 to raise money for FFC. Similar events sponsored by American Freedom for Hunger, along with the Young People of Harvard University, and Young World Development raised $21,000 and $120,000, respectively. FFC purchased 640 acres and farm equipment with these proceeds.[75]

Crucially, major funders supported FFC's need to be governed locally. As NCNW's 1969 annual report summed up the issue, "NCNW is convinced that much of the success of the program stems from the constant involvement, identification and coordination with local community leadership. Thus, County Coordinators have been selected by NCNW and community representatives to maintain this liaison between the communities and national organization."[76] Measure for Measure shared this point of view. An internal document stated, "Our role has been one of aid and support: we set up no programs, push no plans; we seek to meet needs as expressed by local black leadership."[77]

THE DEMISE OF FFC

In 1971, several tornadoes hit Sunflower County. FFC members concentrated their efforts on disaster relief in response. Measure for Measure reprimanded the organization for allocating monies for disaster relief that should have been used to purchase the seeds needed for the growing season. These events were the first inklings of the cooperative's unraveling over the next few years.

In spite of the setbacks the tornadoes represented, the organization continued to provide meaningful assistance. In 1972, member families planted and harvested three hundred acres of cotton, 209 acres of soybeans, and eighty acres of wheat, and they were able to feed thousands in the community with the vegetables they grew on fifty-one acres of land. FFC assisted forty families with their application to FmHA that year. All but two received funding. The organization assisted thirty-five families with funding for deposits on two-, three-, and four-bedroom homes. Thirteen families successfully applied for grants in the amount of eighty-two dollars each to make their mortgage payment.[78] In 1973, FFC had six hundred acres in crop production, three hundred families were recipients of animals from the pig bank, and seventy families were living in the organization's low-income, affordable housing.

FFC distributed scholarships to local high school students to attend college and supported the start of several black businesses.

But donor funds began to dry up. The United States had plunged into an economic downturn, and existing donors had far less to give. The board of directors decided that FFC's survival depended on a massive reorganization in 1972. The social service programs consumed a considerable amount of the organization's attention and funding. Until the farm was financially capable of "independent operation . . . [and] sustaining its own existence," the social service programs would be ended.[79] The part-time professional staff would become full-time so that it could manage both the farm operations and the social programs. Additionally, the board deemed it necessary to engage financial and management services for audits and management suggestions and recommendations.[80]

In late 1972 and early 1973, farmers in the Mississippi Delta experienced droughts and floods, which caused a tremendous crop loss. The sequence was disastrous, as harvesting the few crops that survived the drought from drenched soil was complicated. FFC became unable to pay its seasonal employees. Letters to funders described crops that rotted in the fields because there was no one to harvest them. All told, floods destroyed fifty acres of cotton and soybeans. As a result, the organization stopped farming altogether. FFC could not make payments on its mortgages, its biggest expense, without the cash crops.

A mere four years after the successful launch of the pig bank, FFC closed down its operations. It had not survived long enough to become independent of financial support of grants and donations. The organization sought federal funding from the USDA and other entities that supported antipoverty programs and strategies. The Interreligious Foundation for Community Organization, the Commission on Religion and Race of the United Methodist Church, and FFC's former funder Measure for Measure declined appeals for support. A staunch supporter of Freedom Farm until the end, Harry Belafonte sent out another letter in order to raise funds, but to no avail.

In August 1974, FFC's business manager suffered a fatal heart attack. Hamer also fell ill. At the age of fifty-seven, she was suffering from high blood pressure, diabetes, and fluid retention.[81] Losing her as a fund-raiser and an inspiration was devastating. The board established the Fannie Lou Hamer Foundation to provide funding for FFC; for the emergency and medical programs, to which they were deeply committed; and to offer scholarships and other financial assistance to the children of farm families to further their education. Nevertheless, FFC had to sell its land to pay overdue state and county taxes in 1976. The dream of a self-sufficient agrarian community was over.

The Lessons of Freedom Farm

The civil rights movement was successful in dismantling many oppressive Jim Crow policies. It extended voting privileges to African Americans and enforced desegregation of educational and public facilities. These moves all challenged the power structure of rural southern counties. Nevertheless, in the context of the simultaneous decline of the cotton industry, the powerful maintained the status quo in states such as Mississippi by other means: exacerbating the conditions of poverty; providing inferior education, inadequate health care, and precarious housing; and ignoring high unemployment and the lack of access to healthy food. Illustrating their blatant racial hostility and greed, members of the regional and local white power structure obstructed federal efforts to respond to the severe conditions of poverty. They used these conditions of deprivation as strategies of oppression to maintain their political, economic, and social control and to keep the black majority from mobilizing politically.

As an organic intellectual, Fannie Lou Hamer identified the shift in tactics to keep black Mississippians politically and economically disenfranchised, and she responded to it with efforts to provide a basic quality of life. As the leaders of FFC formed a cooperative intentional community—with housing, employment, educational opportunities, health care, and access to healthy food—they enacted a strategy of commons as praxis. In insisting on self-governance and collaborative decision-making, FFC implemented a prefigurative politics. And through community gardens, the pig bank, and many other projects, FFC developed the kinds of economic autonomy that were a critical foundation for this self-determined, politically engaged, liberated community.

Many civil rights historians, biographers, and journalists have often ignored, missed, or dismissed the contributions of Freedom Farm Cooperative, or they have concentrated on its failures. FFC created an oasis of self-reliance and self-determination in a landscape of oppression maintained in part by deprivation. While it is important to analyze the problems that ultimately led to the demise of the organization in 1975, we should not undervalue its successes. Given its time, scope, intention, and liberatory vision, as well as the fact that this vision was enacted within a pervasively oppressive and racially hostile environment, the movement—while relatively short lived—was a manifestation of self-reliance and the capacity of a community to come together for the provision of food, housing, shelter, education, health care, and employment. This radical experiment constituted an important chapter in the black freedom movement. The organizing strategies of black farmworkers in the 1960s offer lessons that are important today for families displaced by the automobile industry and for others in urban areas currently struggling to access healthy food, adequate and affordable housing, clean water, quality education, health care, and employment. FFC developed a model of community resilience and collective agency as a foundation for political action that speaks to those who live in food-insecure communities such as in Detroit, Milwaukee, Chicago, and New Orleans. It offers a new way for those who have historically been excluded to build sustainable communities.

3

Bypass the Middlemen and Feed the Community

North Bolivar County Farm Cooperative

If a man is able to feed himself, he votes the way he wants to. Not only is this true, but he does anything else he wants to. —William Harrison

When sixty-four residents of Bolivar County met in Rosedale, Mississippi, to organize what would become the North Bolivar County Farm Cooperative (NBCFC) in December 1967, the massive post–World War II migration had taken a significant toll on the area.[1] Bolivar residents were among the nation's most impoverished. As in other parts of Mississippi, employment in agriculture had declined sharply in Bolivar.[2] The people who conceived NBCFC as a means to feed their community by sharing agricultural skills and strategies as well as resources and as a means to create jobs were holdouts—people determined to stay in Mississippi in spite of pressure to move north.

The vast majority of the NBCFC's members had worked as tenant farmers, sharecroppers, day laborers, or domestic workers. The mechanization of agriculture, and federally funded conservation initiatives that paid wealthy white landowners to leave the land fallow, had left them unemployed and living in deplorable housing. Malnutrition and attendant ailments were rampant, and education was underresourced. NBCFC was a community response, a commitment to stay on the rich Mississippi Delta soil without starving to death.

This chapter uses the theoretical framework of CACR to understand how another group of black agricultural cooperatives engaged in community development efforts as a strategy of resistance. As regional efforts rooted in networks of community organizations, these cooperatives operated at a scale and level of complexity far greater than FFC. In response to extreme conditions of financial, social, and political oppression, these black farmers created agricultural cooperatives as a space and a place to practice freedom. While their experiences with white politicians, landowners, and merchants left them battered and justifiably frightened, members of these cooperatives also enacted the strategies of prefigurative politics, economic autonomy, and commons as praxis. They demonstrated collective agency and community resilience in working toward and practicing freedom—freedom to participate in the political process, to engage in an economic model that was cooperative and fair, and to exchange ideas and strategies with others who shared their goals. These organizations offered the space—at an expanded scale and scope—to be innovative and to practice a liberated community built upon principles of cooperative living and sustainability.

North Bolivar's History of Resistance and Resilience

NBCFC drew on a proud history of black autonomy in the region. Mound Bayou, located in Bolivar County, was established as an all-black town immediately after the Civil War. Isaiah Montgomery and Charles Banks founded Mound Bayou on a fertile piece of Yazoo-Mississippi Delta land near the railroad tracks. Montgomery had been born into slavery, but Banks, who was an established businessman, had not. In a 1904 article recounting the history of the town, Booker T. Washington called Banks "the most influential Negro business man in the United States" and described Mound Bayou as "the centre of a Negro population more dense than can be found anywhere else outside of Africa."[3] It was, he wrote, a city of "thrift and self-governance" with a "saw mill, a bank, the Farmers' Cooperative Mercantile Company, real estate ventures, a cotton-seed oil mill and other enterprises."[4] He also described it as "a self-governing community," meaning that the African Americans held the political, economic, and social leadership positions in the community.[5]

From an economic point of view, the center of the town's pride was the cotton oil mill. Washington hosted the opening ceremony for the mill on November 26, 1912. Worth $100,000, the mill was, according to advertising, "entirely owned and constructed by Negroes."[6] The town also had its own cooperatives, including a health insurance cooperative and hospital run by the Knights and Daughters of Tabor.[7]

Mound Bayou was widely known as a "Mecca for Black people" and was recognized as the "largest and most prosperous all-black community in the South."[8] August Meier writes, "Black people visited with reverence and while there, experienced a sense of freedom of action they could not obtain in their own communities."[9] African Americans who had to flee their communities because they had angered the white power structure fled to Mound Bayou and found safety.

But Mound Bayou was an island in a sea of racism. Its status as a place of liberty and refuge for African Americans provided opportunities for activism. In 1965, approximately 150 black farmers organized to demand an increase in wages from the Andrews Plantation in Leland, Mississippi, less than an hour southwest of Mound Bayou. The organizers, mostly tractor drivers, called a work stoppage to demand $1.25 an hour in wages.[10] A. L. Andrews fired and evicted every participant in the strike. Protestors established a tent city they called Strike City just outside the plantation. Andrews went to court to demand an injunction to stop them from picketing in front of his property and called on other landowners to send strikebreakers to complete the work. The presence of Mound Bayou helped make this protest possible.

Despite Andrews' victory, resistance was ongoing. In neighboring Washington County, on January 31, 1966, approximately one hundred black landless farmers and their families occupied the recently vacated property of the Greenville Air Force Base in Greenville, Mississippi, with blankets and boxes of food. In a telegram to President Johnson, they wrote, "We are here because we are hungry. We are here because we have no jobs. Many of us have been thrown off the plantations where we worked for nothing all of our lives. We don't want charity. We demand our rights to jobs, so that we can do something with our lives and build us a future."[11] The protestors demanded food, land, job training, and employment. After two days, the Johnson administration accused them of trespassing and sent in soldiers, who physically dragged the protestors off the base, then left them at the gates. The incident brought national attention to the plight of this community and others in the South.[12]

Such protests undoubtedly were part of what prompted Tufts University and the federal Office of Economic Opportunity to create the Tufts-Delta Medical Center in Mound Bayou in November 1967, which was to become a key supporter of NBCFC. While the Tufts-Delta Medical Center owed its origins to a majority white university in Medford, Massachusetts, the center embedded its service deeply in the community by conducting a two-year ethnographic needs assessment of the area before opening its doors. African American health care professionals born in the South but educated in the North staffed the team.[13]

The fact that food deprivation and chronic malnutrition were the most common ailments identified by doctors at the center set the stage for the center's partnership with NBCFC. The Tufts-Delta pharmacies stocked food along with medicines, and practitioners who worked there wrote vouchers for food to be bought at local stores. As Dr. Jack Geiger, one of the cofounders of the Delta Health Institute, wrote, "What we saw was an agricultural people, displaced by mechanization of the cotton fields, sitting on the richest land in the United States with nothing to do, and having to go hungry or purchase food stamps (if they could get past the welfare system) in order to survive."[14] The medical center's ability to garner federal funding made Tufts-Delta an advantageous partner for NBCFC; their active collaboration with members of the community made the partnership compatible with the ideals of collective agency and autonomy on which NBCFC was based.

NBCFC's Approach to Feeding the Community

Residents of Bolivar County came together as a community to respond to the conditions of poverty that residents experienced as a result of the decline in the agricultural industry. According to the project director, John Hatch, "The cooperative really began as an effort to improve the diets of many of the poor families in northern Bolivar County."[15] Determined to create a measure of self-sufficiency through agriculture, Hatch describes the process of deciding to develop a cooperative: "It seemed to make sense to think in terms of at least growing those items of food that can be grown in this region and making them available to our members. . . . We originally began to discuss the idea of a cooperative food growing effort."[16]

NBCFC restricted membership to those who lived in North Bolivar County and to families whose earnings were less than $1,000 per year. The organization set dues on a sliding scale and allocated jobs according to need, giving preference to the unemployed. David Dulaney and Edward Scott, two black landowners, permitted the cooperative to access to their land for their crops. Isaac Daniel, a local minister and landowner, loaned his tools.[17]

During its first year of operations, nobody who worked at NBCFC received pay. Consequently, members, who had other jobs, accomplished most of the work late at night or on weekends. But the organization successfully purchased seed and rented tractors, and by the end of the first year, 953 families had joined.[18] By the summer of 1968, NBCFC was growing food on 120 acres of leased and borrowed land from regional black landowners. In 1968, the cooperative raised and distributed over one million pounds of produce that included sweet and Irish potatoes, a variety of greens, snap and butter beans, black-eyed peas, and cantaloupes.

The founders of the NBCFC divided the northern part of Bolivar County into twelve sections. Each section elected two representatives who served as members of the board of directors. A management committee oversaw the day-to-day operations. An organizing and screening committee connected the section offices with the cooperative headquarters, and a labor committee conducted employment searches, subject to approval by vote of the membership.[19] Each section had its own cooperative store to sell co-op grown produce. These stores operated with volunteers and a hired staff.[20] With the help of Measure for Measure—the organization that provided key funding to Freedom Farm Cooperative—NBCFC distributed used clothing for children so that they could attend school regularly.

The farm manager determined the work required at each location, and each community took responsibility for gathering the necessary labor. As the organization's progress report described it, "One week all the labor might come from Alligator, the next week it might come from Rosedale, and on like that until the job is done."[21] Cooperative members who worked in the fields typically earned four dollars per day and six dollars in produce. Although fieldworkers received free food, the meeting minutes of the cooperative note, "If a person with a fair job joined the co-op, we could not tell him he could work for all his food. But we can set the rules so that he can buy for a lot less than he has been paying. He could buy the food at just what it costs to make it and get it to him."[22] A recruitment letter by one of the NBCFC's founders, John Hatch, describes how the cooperative drew on the strengths of different members:

> Since most of us know something about farm work, it makes sense for us to try to grow some of our food. But some of us don't have the land. Some of us need help on how to grow vegetables. And some of us don't have all the things it takes to can. So, some of us got together and decided that we might be able to do this in a big way. We asked experts in vegetable farming to help us pick the right land for vegetables. We asked experts on foods to help us pick the most important foods. And we asked experts in canning to help us plan a canning plant that would can enough for our needs. We figure that there are about 3,000 families in North Bolivar County that really need this kind of help. Maybe you[rs is] one.[23]

After the success of NBCFC's first year, Hatch wrote in an annual review that the organization had determined it could produce "quality vegetables here in the Delta, that we can responsibly manage our resources, and that there is economic potential of the food industry perhaps as a source of employment to our people."[24] With this in mind, the NBCFC signed a contract with Heinz Foods for the purchase of fifty acres of cucumbers and began discussions with a new processing plant located in Morehead City, North Carolina. Hatch's annual review described plans for a small canning facility that NBCFC would operate on a community basis, aimed primarily at feeding members but with the idea of selling excess locally.[25]

While NBCFC had hierarchical elements no doubt because of its scale and multiple local centers of leadership that had to also be organized cooperatively that allowed it to function, it was committed to community governance, holding periodic community listening sessions to decide what crops to grow. One purpose of these listening sessions was to gauge interest in particular food crops. Based on this feedback and input from the Tufts-Delta Medical Center physicians, who provided information about which crops offered the greatest nutritional benefit, NBCFC created the Food and Nutrition Cooperative Project. Based on considerations such as soil type, climate, and environment, they selected crops from four categories. The first included vegetable sources of protein. Cooperative documents highlighted the need on the part of children and expectant mothers for crops such as peanuts, lima beans, snap beans, and southern peas. The second category included foods considered high in nutrients and vitamins, such as collard greens, turnip tops, sweet potatoes, tomatoes, okra, and cucumbers. A generation earlier, George Washington Carver had identified the foods in these first two categories as necessary to provide a well-balanced diet for families on a budget. The third category of crops included carbohydrate or staple foods, such as Irish potatoes and corn. The last included fruits such as watermelons and cantaloupes that tend to grow well in the Delta.

While the initial objective of the co-op was to respond to the urgent needs created by unemployment, hunger, homelessness, and other social ills associated with poverty, its programs had a politicizing effect. Over time, leaders such as Hatch began to interrogate their relationship to the means of production within the food system. A letter encouraging community participation in NBCFC exemplifies this. Hatch, a co-executive director at the time, wrote:

All of our lives all we'd ever been able to do was to harvest the raw material, carry it to the white man for the final processing and we began to think too why we get 4 cents a pound for snap beans when delivered to the wholesaler and walk around the corner and find them selling on the fresh market for 25 cents a pound and find them in frozen packages 10 ounces for 30 cents. So it was pretty obvious to us that somebody who handled this product after we unloaded it and before it goes to the eventual consumer, was making some money and it appeared to us that they were making a lot more money than we'd ever make if all we ever did was produce and depend on someone else processing.[26]

The cooperative decided to begin processing its own food to remove the middleman (intermediaries).

NBCFC members were not just concerned about meeting the food needs of those who lived in Bolivar County, but also with supporting and providing food for others whose experiences were similar to theirs. In October 1968, they signed a contract with the newly established civil rights community at Freedom City, mentioned earlier, to provide produce to residents.

The NBCFC's leadership began to advance the idea that a significant market for traditional southern food existed in the North. African American migrants from the South seemed a likely target audience. As one cooperative member said in a meeting, "If you could market Chinese food, Italian food and Jewish food and Irish food in the grocery stores around the country, why couldn't you market a food aimed primarily at the tastes of black people?"[27] Sophisticated techniques for providing such food in the frozen food aisle were far in the future, but the technologies needed to place foods in the canned food aisle seemed within reach. Marketing soul food to migrants from the South seemed like a lucrative proposition.

Like Freedom Farm, NBCFC established several other businesses as well. The Cleveland Sewing Coop made dashikis and leather bags that were sold through the cooperative's stores and placed in co-ops as far away as Madison, Wisconsin.[28] Co-op members discussed creating beauty shops, service stations, sewing centers, and ice cream parlors. They were also actively engaged in organizing a housing development to replace the dilapidated homes that many lived in.[29]

Conclusion

Whereas Freedom Farm was a local effort and based upon the work of its charismatic leader, Fannie Lou Hamer, North Bolivar County Farmers Cooperative was a regional effort and was rooted in a complex of community organizations that supported its programs. Nevertheless, NBCFC was similar to FFC in its use of agriculture as a strategy of self-determination and self-reliance. NBCFC efforts to provide for the community used strategies of commons as praxis in its sharing of resources, and of prefigurative politics in its democratic practices. The organization sought to build economic autonomy that would free farmer-members from the oppressive political-economic relationships of a regional economy run by white elites. As the next chapter shows, these experiences were not unique but reflected a broader cooperative movement that was sweeping the entire region.

4

Agricultural Self-Determination on a Regional Scale

The Federation of Southern Cooperatives

The cooperative movement found its birth in necessity; the necessity of poor black people to combine their resources, talent, [and] labor to make an economic unit able to survive in an economically hostile environment. Cooperatives sprung up throughout the south—from Texas to Virginia. They were varied in their type, e.g., manufacturing, farming, cut and sew, consumers. These cooperatives were operated by the disadvantaged of the south: the blacks, Spanish speaking minorities and a few whites. We organized these combinations of poor people to raise ourselves out of poverty. —Annual report of the Federation of Southern Cooperatives, 1976–77

The monumental accomplishments of the civil rights movement did not include creating a safety net or a jobs program for African Americans who lived in the Jim Crow South as agriculture virtually collapsed in the late 1960s. Yet as Wendell Paris, one of the early leaders of the Federation of Southern Cooperatives (FSC) told me in an interview, "The cooperative movement was an outgrowth of the civil rights movement."[1] In what *The Nation* called "the Poor People's Movement,"[2] cooperatives like Freedom Farm Cooperative and North Bolivar County Farmers Cooperative spread in the late 1960s. Like Martin Luther King's Poor People's Campaign, the cooperatives moved beyond the prevalent emphasis on civil rights and voting rights to address economic injustice, lack of jobs, disparate wealth, and an absence of opportunity for self-determined economics and businesses. Both movements recognized that addressing economic inequality and developing economic independence were intertwined with de jure and legal rights to access public accommodations and the right to vote.[3]

Throughout the rural parts of the country, African American landowners, farmworkers, tenant farmers, sharecroppers, day laborers, and domestic workers organized collectively to obtain the basic necessities of life. In doing so, they resisted the poverty and oppression that spurred the northern and western migration while fighting for equal access to the right to vote and other forms of political empowerment. They drew on the apparatuses that had supported the civil rights movement in the South, including networks of churches and community organizations.

Agriculture was a key element of their cooperative strategy. In many respects, the southern cooperative movement of the late 1960s occupied a territory between the civil rights movement and the Black Power movement. Both movements used strategies of political education, sit-ins, marches, and protests. The overlapping and burgeoning Black Power movement, an ideological stance that previously existed, added to these educational strategies an ideology of self-sufficiency and self-determination[4], which while often developed in urban contexts[5], was consistent with what this book refers to as the principles of CACR and was adapted by landless agrarians. The networking and organizational skills that were essential for movement organizing of the civil rights movement were thus channeled to create working-class freedom organizations, such as agricultural cooperatives. In these cooperatives, black workers drew on the skills they had used in growing cash crops for white landowners to create organizations that spoke to the liberatory impulses of the day, the oppressive forces of economic discrimination, as well as their dire needs.[6] They grew food crops for themselves as a basis for political autonomy.

Like NBCFC and FFC, FSC focused on developing autonomy for former tenant farmers and sharecroppers. But its member cooperatives also introduced innovations in environmental conservation and in sustainable crop production. They also developed mechanisms for multistate collective organizing that transcended, both in scale and scope, what had gone before. In this way, members created a new model for how self-determination could be pursued.

FSC began in 1967 at a meeting in Mount Beulah, Mississippi. In December of that year, twenty-two representatives of southern rural cooperatives came together to discuss remedies for the extreme poverty their members faced. Albert J. McKnight, an African American Catholic priest based in Louisiana, and John Zippert, a civil rights organizer with CORE, arranged the meeting. McKnight's work with cooperatives and on behalf of impoverished black communities in the South was legendary. He began developing cooperatives as a response to poverty in 1964 with the Southern Consumers Cooperative, a "statewide investment group that encouraged members to invest, save, offered member families low interest loans and provided political education about the importance of cooperatives." He claimed that the SCC was the "first low income cooperative in the South in modern times."[7] Ultimately, McKnight brought together over 2,000 low-income citizens in cooperatives throughout the South, mostly in Louisiana.[8]

FSC's founding documents describe the organization as "an umbrella organization building a network of cooperative institutions in the southeast. It serves as a resource development center by raising funds and providing technical assistance to its members. By addressing itself to policy issues and lobbying on behalf of its membership, the Federation is the principal advocate for low income cooperative development in this country."[9] In the words of its mission statement, FSC was created "to assist southern rural communities to build and sustain themselves through collective action."[10] Organizers were committed to galvanizing economic development for black farmers, landowners, and rural communities.

The objectives of the Federation were to develop cooperatives and credit unions, to protect and expand the landholdings of black family farmers in the South, and to "develop, advocate for, and support public policies to benefit the members of black and other family farmers and low income rural communities."[11] The Federation became known as the "co-op of co-ops." It offered bookkeeping, technical and financial services, resource development, and training in agricultural skills.[12] The developers of the cooperative were aware of the complex and interconnected challenges black farmers faced. In their words: "Although the problems were diverse, the goals were the same: to raise ourselves out of poverty by working together, pooling resources for the most effective and desirable economic growth."[13]

The founding members of the Federation were rooted in southern communities and committed to identifying solutions and providing resources that would ultimately allow their communities to provide for themselves. They had an intimate knowledge of community needs. To meet these community-identified needs, the Federation successfully submitted grants to the Office of Economic Opportunity and private donors to bring in experts for training in the mechanics of effective cooperatives as well to support members of communities who wanted to put this training into action. While a lack of technical and business skills had arguably created problems for Freedom Farm, FSC set out to teach record keeping, business planning, and other technical skills. Cooperative leaders who received training at FSC headquarters could take these skills back to their home communities to improve the functioning of their cooperatives. Early on, they identified the need to create a center for conducting extensive classroom training, demonstrating farming strategies, and to organizing and producing organizational materials. The objective was to help black farmers purchase land and maintain ownership for agricultural purposes at a time when land speculators and developers drove up property taxes, and to offer alternative channels to obtain both land and farm supplies.[14]

As if influenced by Du Bois, members of the Federation followed the Rochdale Principles, which were developed in 1844 by the Rochdale Society of Equitable Pioneers in England and adopted by the International Co-operative Alliance. The principles establish that equitable treatment and operation were key principles of the cooperatives. All member cooperatives of the Federation also adopted these principles, which called for "open membership, democratic membership control (one member, one vote), limited return on investment, patronage refunds to participation, constant education, [and] constant expansion."[15] Thus, they prioritized cooperative work and collective responsibility. The Federation had separate associations in each of the states where it operated, and most decisions were made at the state level.[16] According to the 1971 annual report, Federation leaders envisioned a future in which each association would have a program committee, a fund-raising committee, and an education committee.[17]

The events that led to the acquisition of the land for the Federation headquarters is a story of resistance in its own right.[18] In 1970, dozens of black farmers who worked on the Rogers plantation in Sumter County, Alabama, filed a lawsuit against the owner of the plantation, Barnes Rogers, for two reasons. One reason was because he had denied them the cotton subsidy check the federal government had paid for work they completed, in spite of his clear legal obligation to do so.[19] The second was that Rogers evicted them and their families from the land for exercising the right to vote. The families organized themselves as the Panola Land Buying Cooperative and approached the Federation for help in purchasing land for housing and farming. As a result of this concerted action, the Federation worked with a number of other nonprofit organizations dedicated to the well-being of southern farmers to negotiate a deal to purchase 901 acres of land for $135,000.[20]

By 1974, just seven years after its founding, 134 cooperatives had joined FSC from fourteen southern states.[21] The Federation served a particularly large population in the Alabama Black Belt, where its cooperative members ranged from a handicraft co-op with twelve members to the Southwest Alabama Farmers' Cooperative Association (SWAFCA), an organization that included more than 2,000 families in ten counties in 1974.[22] SWAFCA's membership was 97 percent African American, with the racial makeup of the remainder varying by state.[23]

The Federation's central staff provided training to association staff as well as to members, created educational materials, and made loans to community members. Members paid back some of these loans through labor, the value of which was calculated at fair wages. FSC was sensitive to the barriers members faced in obtaining resources.[24] Farmers who could not read could not apply for loans, grants, or assistance on their own behalf. In order to provide these much-needed kinds of support, staff sought federal funding from the Office of Economic Opportunity (OEO).

Both Freedom Farm Cooperative and North Bolivar County Farmers Cooperative received assistance from FSC at different points in their development. Using federal and private funding, the umbrella organization made it possible for landless farmers to access land and develop small farm cooperatives. It trained and retrained them in agricultural technology, farm management, and energy consumption, facilitated cooperative purchasing and marketing, and provided employment opportunities. It also offered educational experiences, both in the field and in their own training center, on the new technologies for crop production and livestock operations and linked all of these efforts to investments in small-scale enterprises.

FSC's Agricultural Programs

FSC's 1974–75 annual report lamented, "Many have written off the small farmer and left him and his family enterprise to sink or swim in an economic climate that runs counter to his very existence." In contrast, the report continued, "the Federation has always believed that small farms, family farms, have their rightful and productive place in American agriculture." A third of the cooperatives that made up the Federation were agricultural, the largest of any of its sectors. Many of the black farmers in these cooperatives were landless; they lived and worked on plantations whites owned, or they rented land from white owners. Many of those owners objected to their tenants affiliating with the Federation and evicted them when they learned of their involvement.[25]

FSC was committed to the uplift of these farmworkers through such programs as the Small Farmers School Program, which offered information and training in farm management, financial management, purchasing and marketing, livestock maintenance and training, and crop diversification. It introduced new crops to farmers who had produced cotton all their lives, including cash crops such as cucumbers, and instructed them to plant fall vegetables and harvest two crops per year instead of the single crop, cotton, that had sustained them previously.[26] This was a powerful way of increasing incomes for small farmers. The program promoted sustainable practices such as water irrigation and catchment systems and hoop houses for season extension. It also provided information on programs and land grant institution services.[27] Consistent with Carver, it trained cooperative members in soil nutrient samples; fertilizer analysis; farm record keeping; seed-bed preparation; seed selection; new technologies in planting, weeding, harvesting, and processing; and equipment maintenance. FSC also taught sustainable forestry and ran a series of youth programs that encouraged young people to become skilled farmers. Members came to the training center in Epes, sometimes supported by Federation stipends, to learn at the organization's demonstration farms. The farm operations included beef cattle, pigs, poultry, vegetables, soybeans, and grains. The income from these operations went toward employee wages, to pay off the mortgage on the Federation property, and to fund FSC services. FSC offered farm visits and group tours to members and the interested public.[28] For a minority of black landowners, FSC also provided legal advice on the transmission and distribution of landownership to heirs following the death of the primary landowner.

Distributors of agricultural inputs—such as seeds, fertilizers, pesticides, implements, and other farm-related supplies—in the South, as well as plantation owners, had long profited from exploitative relationships built upon the racial hierarchy. FSC broke the hold of this system. Members of the Federation knew that they were being exploited when they purchased inputs at plantation stores and sold their goods to local merchants. They could see the great difference between the prices they received from the buyer and the prices at which those goods were sold in the market. Through its programs, FSC replaced the middlemen and thereby maximized profit for the small farmers.[29] This strategy of eliminating the middlemen extended after harvest as well. FSC was committed to returning profits to the farmers instead of using produce buyers and brokers, who profited inordinately from the labor of those who worked the land by paying the lowest possible amount to seemingly desperate farmers. Buying and selling in bulk enabled cooperative members to negoti-

Rev. Wendell Paris, Federation of Southern Cooperatives' training center in Epes, Alabama. Photo by Patricia Goudvis.

ate a better price. Thus, a larger proportion of profits went to the farmers, to supporting their continued training, and to providing funding for the Federation and its offices. One cooperative found that its members' profits doubled after it made the change.[30]

The Fertilizer and Farm Supply Purchasing Program assisted coop members with acquiring farm supplies, effectively breaking the monopoly of the exploitative plantation commissary for tenant farmers and sharecroppers. The Federation's program offered bulk sales and a loan/credit program. These low- or no-cost loans allowed farmers to purchase supplies against the eventual profits from their crops, offering them the opportunity to get out of debt. FSC offered almost everything that a farmer needed—from seeds; to fertilizer and lime; to automotive supplies such as tires and oil; to tillers, sprayers, dusters, and fence-making supplies; to feed for livestock and veterinary supplies.[31] Members also relied on the Federation for capital or guarantees needed to purchase fertilizer and farm supplies from wholesale dealers.[32]

Young farmer feeding cattle at the Federation of Southern Cooperatives' training center in Epes, Alabama. Photo by Patricia Goudvis.

The Federation identified the provision of sufficient farm supplies on a timely basis at reasonable prices as one of its most important functions. In the words of an FSC staff member in the organization's 1974–75 annual report, "Synchronizing the production, harvesting, marketing functions relative to small farmers is getting at the very essence of what cooperation, i.e., cooperatives, is all about. It is foolish to even suggest that small farmers can exist over the long run without creating associations—without working together, pooling productive, purchasing and marketing power."[33]

One of FSC's member cooperatives was the Mid-South Oil Cooperative. A group of black tenant farmers formed this co-op when white landowners refused to sell oil to them after they registered to vote. Wendell Paris tells the story:

A number of us recognized that something more than social action was called for. We needed economic development to sustain our communities that were coming under attack now that many had ventured to change their social condition. For example, in Tennessee in a four-county area close to Memphis, a number of black farmers decided to register to vote. When they did, the fuel suppliers refused to sell them gasoline, so they had to bootleg it. They were forced to drive into Memphis and bring back cans of gas in the back of their cars so they could plant their crops. So that's how they set up the first cooperative in the area with the farmers selling each other gasoline.[34]

Once the Mid-South Oil Cooperative joined the Federation, with a membership reaching 250 in just four years, FSC could facilitate exchanges of oil among member coops when some of them had surpluses and others had shortfalls.[35] FSC would also buy in bulk from distributors and make oil and other inputs available to member coops at or near cost. During the 1974–75 growing season, when fertilizer prices spiked due to the 1973 oil embargo, FSC made it possible for cooperatives under its umbrella to exchange fertilizers. FSC documents called these exchanges "cooponomics."[36]

The 1970s energy crisis brought exorbitant fees for fossil fuels as well as shortages. FSC responded by promoting small farm energy and conservation efforts that emphasized greenhouses for season extension and the use of solar energy on the farm. It also promoted water conservation measures, such as irrigation, retention, and catchment systems. Members learned to build woodstoves from recycled materials to heat their homes and barns, a practice the Federation adopted for its own offices and stores because of the high price of gas and electricity. They constructed and put into operation fourteen solar greenhouses. They also provided instructional materials and other educational materials detailing woodstove construction and greenhouse design.

In keeping with its energy conservation practices, FSC provided a market analysis for new crops that required fewer fossil fuel inputs during cultivation. It provided loans against energy savings to members to help them implement alternatives to burning fossil fuels.

Understanding the cost-prohibitive nature of many of these energy-saving techniques, the Federation provided what the organization's annual report termed a "revolving loan fund designed to be self-perpetuating," explaining that "this fund makes no interest loans to participants so that they can make energy-related improvements to their coop buildings and homes. As the loans are paid back (usually as a result of energy savings or greenhouse plant sales) the fund is replenished and other loans are made."[37]

Once the crops were harvested, members of the Federation identified markets as another point of exploitation. Buyers and brokers had the upper hand when individual farmers sold them their crops, usually in small amounts. They offered extraordinarily low prices because they knew farmers had no alternatives. To resolve this, FSC led many farmers to consolidate their harvests and to bargain with the buyers collectively. This increased their bargaining power and allowed them to sell at higher prices. The Federation identified food processors who might buy their crops; ultimately, it built its own processing plant. Whether a farmer brought in a single gunny sack or a truckload of produce, FSC would collect it and transport it to processors and chain-store buyers in cities such as Memphis, Jackson, Mobile, Montgomery, and Birmingham, and to places as far away as Wisconsin and Michigan. It would then return most of its profit to the farmers and use the remainder to fund FSC services. One farmer-member explained, "A man can't come in to market with a basket of beans because the market has gotten sophisticated and there is no way to handle a transaction of that kind. A truckload of beans is a different story. You can sell that in a minute and get a good price for it. By gathering up the beans from a number of farmers, basket by basket, and selling them as a truckload we get a better price."[38]

Farmers coordinated their production so that FSC could collect large quantities of produce and achieve efficiencies of scale. FSC's marketing manual quotes a farmer from Flint River Farmer's Cooperative in southwest Georgia on the negotiation process:

Well, first of all we sit down and discuss what we want to grow. And then each of us grows a portion of, say, collard greens. If we decide to grow 10 or 20 acres of collard greens, each individual will grow a certain amount of acres. Like, I might grow one acre and then two or three weeks later another farmer might grow an acre and then we pass it around. That way it won't all be ready at the same time and we can have produce year round. That's the same way we grow the peas. We rotate.[39]

By 1974, FSC served 10,000 small farmers organized in over thirty agricultural cooperatives, providing marketing, purchasing, and technical assistance. The annual report to members stated, "Our members collectively own half a million acres of land; over $7 million of vegetables, soybeans, livestock, and cotton were sold through these coops last year; the co-ops make it possible for small farmers with an average of less than 50 acres to retain and make productive their small land-holdings."[40] By 1977, FSC farmers controlled over one million acres of land throughout the South. They cultivated more than 20,000 acres of vegetables, 200,000 acres of soybeans and feed grains, and several thousand acres of cotton. They also held 100,000 acres or more in improved pastures for livestock. The 1976–77 annual report described the joint marketing and purchasing associations as "an initial step" toward "maximizing the collective productive wealth of the community resources."[41]

In addition to agricultural cooperatives, FSC included nonagricultural food-based cooperatives such as ones in the fishing industry. Some coops were involved in shrimping, while others experimented with aquaponics and farmed catfish as a way to raise fish sustainably and to produce fertilizer. This innovative industry fed into food provisioning and small business development projects. But fish were only the tip of the iceberg. A list of innovative projects from one of FSC's publications included "channel catfish production (in ponds and raceways), irrigated vegetable production (using machinery adaptable to small farmers), green house production of off-season vegetables, flowers, shrubs and transplants; and a general row crop component to raise feed and pasture for the livestock components."[42]

In 1979, the Federation expanded its reach by collaborating with like-minded organizations. These included the Emergency Land

Fund, a southern-based nonprofit organization formed in 1973 to address the issue of black land loss, and the Southern Cooperative Development Fund, a funding agency that provided emergency loans to struggling cooperatives.[43] The three organizations created a joint program called the Consortium for the Development of the Rural Southeast. This program worked with 225 agricultural producers in five states, providing a fifteen-week training program and paying the attendees for their time.[44]

In addition to supporting member coop agricultural enterprises, the Federation was able to provide assistance to member cooperatives with other economic activities, including marketing, purchasing, bookkeeping, and "field accounting," which involved audit reports and tax preparation.[45] The Federation also offered several management-training programs and classes in cooperative economics. It supported the development of different kinds of cooperatives, including consumer, marketing, supply, and service coops. It supported communities in the transition from buying clubs to full-fledged supermarkets, and it helped establish credit unions and handicraft, housing, fishing, and light manufacturing cooperatives that encouraged sewing, metal stamping, bakery, and the manufacturing of building materials.[46]

Housing, Health, and Social Programs

In addition to the programs that provided economic support to the cooperatives, FSC provided housing to displaced farmers; according to the 1970 census, Sumter County had more units of substandard housing than standard ones. Most of these units lacked indoor plumbing and properly functioning chimneys.[47] Like Freedom Farm Cooperative, FSC trained agricultural workers to plan housing developments and make site preparations, including constructing sewage systems, building homes, and remodeling. FSC's 1969 annual report noted that there were "over one million substandard housing units [that] remain occupied in the rural south," and resolved that "these deplorable housing condition[s] . . . should, must and will be eradicated.[48] One of the Federation's coop members, the Simpson County Development Project, completed the construction of thirty rental units, along with a co-op center for educational and recreational services, and operated a co-op general store.

FSC developed and operated the Black Belt Family Health Care Center at the Rural Research, Training, and Demonstration Center in Epes, Alabama. This ambulatory preventative health care cooperative employed a primary care physician and a nurse practitioner and provided laboratory test analysis, a low-cost pharmacy, and X-ray services to residents of the Alabama Black Belt at prices on a sliding scale. A program to train nurses and physicians in treating the specific health needs of impoverished patients never got off the ground. White local, medical providers were to blame. Viewing the health care center as competition, they enlisted their congressional representatives and senators to cut federal funding for the program. As a result, FSC could only provide basic health screenings, nutrition and prenatal counseling, food distribution to expectant mothers, and senior citizen in-home visitation.[49]

If the housing and health-care programs served members' bodies, the Right to Read Program served their minds. The program consisted of both in-home individualized literacy classes and small group classes in schools, libraries, and community centers. Almost 500 members received in-home tutoring. Incarcerated persons received literacy training via satellite television. Members could also access GED training and could earn college credits by attending an exchange program with Miles College–Eutaw.[50] With the assistance of the Miles College library in Birmingham, FSC created a system of ten mini-libraries throughout the Black Belt. In 1973, the Alabama Department of Education licensed FSC as a private vocational school.

Cooperatives as the Basis of
Self-Determination and Resistance

Cooperatives such as those organized by the FSC posed a threat to white power structures—a potent threat in the South where whites were in the numeric minority. As one black southern farmer remarked to a reporter for *Black Enterprise* magazine in 1970,

"The black man who makes his living on his farming isn't likely to sell his vote."[51] Another cooperative member speaking to the same publication about the cooperative movement said, "One of these days maybe we'll own a pickle plant of our own, we could get a lot of people jobs around here, give people security. And if he gets security, a man thinks politically about other things."[52]

An example of the backlash that a member organization experienced is that of the Grand Marie Vegetable Cooperative of Sunset, Louisiana. The cooperative had begun in 1965 when a group of black farmers came together to discuss the difficulties they had accessing agricultural resources. Economic conditions were so dire that they knew they would have to leave the South for employment if the price of sweet potatoes didn't go up. They had sought relief for economic conditions through electoral participation, running for positions on the state's Agricultural Stabilization Conservation Service committee. They were the first black candidates to run for these positions, and none won a seat. They were convinced that there had been electoral fraud and intimidation of sharecropping voters, given the majority-black demographic. The Grand Marie Vegetable Cooperative was successful; it shipped $102,000 worth of sweet potatoes to markets in 1971. Their impact on the market required others to lower their profits in order to obtain sales.

The backlash came in 1972. A group of white sweet potato shippers asked the management at the Guaranty National Bank Service to withhold access to a $60,000 line of credit for which Grand Marie had been approved. The checks that Grand Marie had written, in the understanding that the cooperative had money in the bank, bounced, leaving it in a financially precarious position.[53] Such repression did not end the cooperative movement but encouraged African Americans to increase their involvement in local and regional political organizations.

Drawing on a culture of state's rights that extended from the Civil War and to *Brown v. Board of Education*, local and regional white political officials as well as white business owners sought to destroy the black cooperative movement and its federal financial backing. Plantation owners fired day laborers and put sharecroppers and tenant farmers out of their homes if they participated in coop activities. In a less drastic measure, they forbade them from openly competing with local food processors.

The threat that the white power structures perceived was real. The Federation actively encouraged its membership to participate in local political struggles and concerns. The transition from organizing cooperatives to participation in local politics was clear: "As the self-help concept of cooperation permeates the minds and takes hold in the actions of people, the growth of our cooperative movement is and becomes more truly self-generating and self-perpetuating."[54] The organizing mechanism that allowed black farmers to increase their profits and provide for their livelihoods also educated them on the mechanisms to push back against oppressive political power.

Although it is not clear what role the Federation played in creating the political organization called the Sumter County Coalition, whites in the county thought they knew. As in many of the South's majority black counties, whites controlled the school board, which systematically kept the public schools with a majority black student enrollment impoverished. The Sumter County Coalition led a six-week boycott of schools and businesses in Livingston, the county seat, demanding increased funding for black schools and recruitment of qualified African American instructors and administrators. In response, the county allocated almost half a million dollars to upgrade school facilities and hired a black principal at one of the county schools. The Coalition also worked to ensure that there were African American challengers to oppose the white school board incumbents and supported them in the election process.[55]

The white power structure attacked the Federation in response. Calling the Federation's activities "government funded activism," white political officials charged that its political activity violated federal funding guidelines.[56] Livingston mayor I. Drayton Pruitt Jr. led the attack. He promised his constituents he would return things to the way "they used to be" in southwestern Alabama. In 1979, Pruitt, his father (and law partner) I. Drayton Pruitt Sr., Sumter County probate judge Sam Massingill, and tax assessor Joe Steagall wrote a letter to Alabama congressman Richard Shelby complaining about the federal government's support of FSC. Shelby initiated a preliminary Government Accountability Office audit in response. The audit proved unsuccessful in halting FSC activities.[57] Alabama's white establishment continued to fight FSC. In 1979, a federal grand jury in northern Alabama ordered the Federation to "produce any and all documents in connection with federal funding of FSC and its affiliated cooperatives" for the preceding four years.[58] The investigation involved perusal of ten file-cabinet drawers, including 40,000 cancelled checks, and lasted eighteen months. Although no charges were filed and no evidence of wrongdoing was found, the damage was done. Defending itself cost the Federation $20,000 in legal fees, and a number of funders backed away because of the suspicion of fiscal improprieties.

In an interview, FSC's executive director Charles Prejean described the investigation as "a deliberate attempt on the part of the U.S. Attorney's office and the FBI to destroy the entire organization, without going into any reason for this action."[59] FSC cofounder John Zippert concurred: "The White politicians are really disturbed that Blacks stuck together during the school boycott. They looked for a scapegoat and decided on the Federation. . . . We may be a catalyst, but we are not directly involving ourselves in political matters in Sumter County. It's only natural that when people realize the problems facing them they begin to think politically. But our interest is in developing cooperatives for poor people, not in ripping off federal monies."[60]

With its fundraising relationships damaged, FSC had no possibility of making up the deficit. Contending with the loss of funding, Sumter County coalition leader Wendell Paris[61] told the journal *Southern Changes*, "We're not going to roll over and play dead. We are going to obtain some control over our lives here. Mayor Pruitt and his daddy and other whites who run this county have run this county long enough. Black folks are in the majority here and we intend to fight for what is rightfully ours. We want to make this a better community for everyone."[62] Despite racially motivated legal and political attacks, similar to Du Bois' sentiment regarding the potential of cooperatives in segregated spaces, FSC continued to work toward its vision that African Americans would "one day own our own supermarkets, department stores, automobile franchises and eventually, become manufacturers of automobiles and the like. We must own our own drugstores, bakeries, hardware stores and other industrial services needed to make our communities as self-contained as possible."[63]

In another example of the power of black cooperatives and the threat they posed to the white economic and political power structure, members of SWAFCA experienced blatant attacks on their ability to move produce from the farm to market. White business owners organized to refuse to sell SWAFCA members supplies or intentionally delayed delivery of their purchases. In at least one case, a processing plant agreed to purchase SWAFCA produce but backed out of the agreement under pressure from local officials.[64] Alabama state troopers stopped a fleet of refrigerated SWAFCA trucks on frivolous grounds, allowed the drivers to leave but, detaining the trucks at the side of the road until they ran out of gas, which caused the cooling mechanism to shut down.[65] Cucumbers rotted in the Alabama heat for hours.

Another incident involving SWAFCA began because the Whitfield Pickle Company and King Pharr Company had been forced to raise the price they paid for peas and cucumbers by 50 percent as a result of SWAFCA's organizing farmers to whom these companies had previously paid exploitative prices.[66] Company executives chartered a jet to Washington, D.C., to protest federal funding granted to SWAFCA via the Office of Economic Opportunity (a federal agency responsible for administering War on Poverty programs).[67] They brought elected officials and probate judges from each of the ten counties where SWAFCA had membership, the entire Alabama congressional delegation, and Governor Lurleen Wallace to the OEO office to convince officials to discontinue the funding. OEO director Sargent Shriver met with the gathered officials but refused to withdraw funds.

Despite the efforts of regional elites to derail their projects, SWAFCA continued its efforts, merging in the mid-1970s with the Federation of Southern Cooperatives (FSC). As the next chapter shows, the efforts to use agriculture as a community-based strategy to improve the lives of its residents would resurface almost fifty years later, in Detroit, the same place that many African Americans fled to, in search of freedom.

A Lasting Legacy

At the time this book went to press, the Federation was still organizing black cooperatives in southern states. Its tenacity and comprehensive approach to creating sustainable agricultural work in order to build, support, and protect economically self-determined communities is a powerful example of CACR. The Federation also serves as a crucial example for communities struggling with developing food systems, employment opportunities, educational institutions, health care, and other measures of community wellness. What Fannie Lou Hamer accomplished in one cooperative and what the North Bolivar County Farmers Cooperative accomplished in a single, significant county, the Federation carried throughout the whole South.

The work of the Federation combines the technical training advocated by Booker T. Washington and George Washington Carver with W. E. B. Du Bois's principles of cooperatives as democratic process. True to the vision of these thinkers, it demonstrates that those with little can pool their resources together to make substantive changes to their lives. It was successful in bringing federal resources to develop and support its member cooperatives. In 2017, FSC celebrated its fiftieth anniversary and continues to support the development of new and existing cooperatives. According to the 2016 annual report, the FSC received funding in that year from thirty private organizations and the USDA.

Some said that the Federation's services were not needed or that they could have been provided by other agencies or organizations such as the USDA Cooperative Extension, the outreach arm of the USDA.[68] But one FSC leader described the importance of the Federation in a way that highlighted the organization's special contributions:

Show us the USDA sponsored facilities that are responsive to the needs of small farmers; show us the facilities that are disseminating information useful to the small farmer in a form and context he [*sic*] can understand; show us the facilities that are oriented toward providing techniques and training to small farmers in enterprises that can produce new income for their families. These facilities do not exist in the South; that is why we are creating our own training institute, centrally located within our membership area and centrally concerned with giving new skills to disadvantaged people in the context of developing a self-help movement for substantive economic changes in our society.[69]

While there were federal programs established to offer support for impoverished residents in rural communities, many of the black land workers in the south could not access these programs, especially after their participation in community organizing or in politics. FSC provided resources for self-determination, offering technical assistance to farmers and workers who had been excluded from educational opportunities and market participation and laying the groundwork needed for economic self-sufficiency.

5

Drawing on the Past toward a Food Sovereign Future

The Detroit Black Community Food Security Network

For more than four centuries, African Americans provided most of the labor for the production of cotton and tobacco—two of the cash crops that generated sizable wealth in the colonies and the nation. While either coerced and unpaid or discriminated against and underpaid, black workers survived under this system. By the middle of the twentieth century, the mechanization of agriculture had reduced the need for this manual labor, leaving black workers unemployed, undereducated, and homeless.

So far, this book has discussed the strategies employed by those who wished to remain in the South during this period—those who stayed on the land. This chapter tells the stories of descendants of those who migrated north, in particular to the Midwest city of De-troit. It describes the new farming practices of the children and grandchildren of those sharecroppers, tenant farmers, domestic workers and farm laborers recruited by Henry Ford to work in his factories there. Like their relatives in the South, these former farmers managed to survive, though their work was dangerous and underpaid compared to that of their white counterparts, and management often exploited them to work as strikebreakers, taking advantage of the racism of the automobile unions. At the same time, coming to Detroit meant joining a rich history of in-novation. From automobiles to music, Detroiters put the world on wheels and, thanks to Motown, provided the music of a genera-tion.[1] The automobile industry catapulted the United States into prosperity after World War II, much as southern agriculture had secured its economy in earlier decades.

For those individuals who made the Great Migration, Detroit's late twentieth-century economic decline might seem like history repeating itself. It began as a result of the urban economic divestment and white flight that followed the Detroit Rebellion of 1967. It continued as international competition in the auto industry led automakers to lower labor costs, outsourcing parts and eventually whole cars to factories in southern states and then other nations. These downward trends culminated in the bankruptcies of General Motors and Chrysler in 2009.

As relative latecomers to employment in the industry, black workers were particularly vulnerable under "last hired, first fired" policies. The collapse of the auto industry left many Detroit workers of all races in search of employment, education, health care, and other resources critical to their well-being, but black workers were hit especially hard.[2]

Immediately after the Detroit Rebellion, whites began to leave the city in large numbers, while African Americans stayed. Black flight followed in the early 2000s, however, as middle-class African Americans began to leave the city for the surrounding no-longer-predominantly-white suburbs and also joined a "reverse migration" back to the South. Like African Americans who had found a way to remain in the South by developing cooperatives, Detroit's remaining black community found a way to resist the pressure to leave by building sustainable communities around agriculture.

For these "new" farmers of Detroit, the legacies of Freedom Farm Cooperative, North Bolivar County Farmers Cooperative, and the Federation of Southern Cooperatives were not only geographically but also chronologically distant. While the founders of the Detroit Black Community Food Security Network (DBCFSN) have not necessarily studied this history, they have reenacted many of the same strategies as a way to resist the racial hierarchy, stay in a place they love, and create conditions necessary for community development and survival. Once again, a community of African Americans who had been dismissed, whose labor had been exploited and discarded, and who struggled to access quality food and other necessities decided to return to the rich legacy of growing food as a strategy of survival and resistance. This chapter explores the work of DBCFSN as a contemporary example of how African Americans are returning to their agricultural roots in order to rebuild community through growing food. One of the most significant demonstrations of the theoretical framework of CACR appears in the city's largest farm in its burgeoning urban agriculture movement.

Organizational Beginnings

When Detroit mayor Coleman A. Young created the federally funded Farm-a-Lot program in 1974, Detroit's population had been declining for over two decades: from almost two million in 1950 to 1.5 million in 1970.[3] Young's goal was to support urban agriculture. Over the next forty years, his vision bore fruit: the community's capacity to grow food to provide for its most vulnerable residents has increased considerably. Today, Detroit is a major site of urban agriculture and community-based food systems. As the contraction of the auto industry and the 2008–2010 foreclosure crisis spurred even greater shrinkage of the population—to less than 700,000 in 2010[4]—public services in Detroit were hit especially hard. The decline in revenue from property taxes resulted in severe cuts to the public school system and other public services, including emergency services such as fire and police, trash and snow removal, and maintenance of water systems. At the same time, rising unemployment caused foreclosures, water shut-offs and homelessness. As a result, the city of Detroit entered the largest municipal bankruptcy in U.S. history in 2013. In this context of massive urban divestment and economic devastation, the foodscape of the city changed. The city's major chain grocery stores closed, abandoning neighborhoods whose residents had the least access to transportation.[5]

This was the situation that Malik Yakini sought to address when he called together about forty community activists in February 2006. Only one major chain grocery store remained in a city that spans approximately 140 square miles. A longtime black-liberation activist and the owner of Black Star Community Bookstore in Detroit, Yakini said his objective was to "raise awareness about food policy to ensure our community was getting the healthiest food possible."[6] Attending the meeting were other longtime activists from Detroit's Black Power era and people who held positions in city government. Yakini called on them to "grasp larger control over the food system and to build self-reliance in our community."[7] Together they established DBCFSN and laid out its goals: education, food access, and collective buying. They saw these as critical strategies to ensure that black Detroiters had what they needed not only to survive but also to thrive.

In explaining why community activists focused on food as a response to the economic devastation that accompanied the loss of automobile industry jobs, Yakini argued that food was simply a basic necessity. Any strategy that sought self-reliance had to have food access as a building block. But also, Yakini noted that food was an issue that united people regardless of their philosophical differences. Because everyone has to eat, food security provided a basis for collaboration that many other goals would not have.

Detroit's urban agriculture movement had been burgeoning since 2000 and attracting international attention. Yet media coverage of the movement, which had started decades earlier with Coleman Young's project, virtually excluded black Detroiters. Newly arrived white college graduates and urban agriculture enthusiasts, many of whom viewed Detroit as a tabula rasa to be reinvented using federal funds and monies gained from nonprofit organizations, dominated media coverage. Their presence also threatened to exclude black grassroots food and agricultural activists by crowding them out of discussions about how the city should respond to the food needs of its residents.

DBCFSN mobilized the black community for self-determination and articulated a community-based response to these newly relocated residents. This mobilization began with conversations about community food sovereignty and security and about offering African Americans a chance to participate in the redevelopment of a city they had long loved. Yakini describes the philosophy and work of the group as rooted in a pan-African philosophy of pride and solidarity that is also antiracist, anticapitalist, and self-determined. The network emphasizes unity throughout the African Diaspora, especially those who live in the Western Hemisphere. Yakini describes the understanding that "everything is everything" as intrinsic to DBCFSN's belief system and pan-African approach. For him, this phrase grounds the organization's ecosystematic approach. Those who work the land are also land stewards. They honor and exemplify the belief that all of life is interconnected. According to Yakini, "Our approach to farming and our approach to land stewardship is related to our interconnectedness to nature, [as] opposed to a more Judeo-Christian western idea that man has dominion over the earth. That frames our agricultural practices and frames our approach to land stewardship and our relationship to the land."[8]

The network's day-to-day work is grounded in an antiracist, anticapitalist mindset and emphasizes cooperative effort and collective wealth-building. Working on the farm is part of political education—the work is rooted in an examination of the systems of economic and racial oppression and their impact on the food system. Creative analyses and alternatives to racist and capitalist systems of interaction are guiding principles of the organization. Through political education and organizing, its members work to dismantle systems and structures of white supremacy. They respond most specifically to the ways that the food system reflects powers of oppression (racism and capitalism) that ultimately determine who can afford to be healthy. They are explicit in emphasizing the impact of capitalism on the food system and how its forces disproportionately restrict African Americans' access to healthy and affordable food. For Yakini, the work of the organization, and most specifically its best-known project, D-Town Farm, "is an example of the possibility, as a powerful symbol to black people around the world . . . to create spaces where we can practice collective work for the common good." For many of its members, DBCFSN stands as a model of community self-determination.

DBCFSN addresses the political and economic structures that distance black people from healthy food in two ways: through action and through conversations among members. Yakini describes the political education DBCFSN offers this way: "Dialogue takes place within the organization but also with those who enter our sphere. Anybody who comes hears something about our analysis of white supremacy and how that functions within the food system. Anyone we partner with is going to hear that analysis. Through that we've been able to contribute to the public discourse about racism and have had an impact on the public consciousness, particularly within the circle of food activists and foodies in Detroit."[9] For DBCFSN, the work and interactions with others are ways to open the community's eyes to the inequities intrinsic to capitalism. Yakini says, "Our efforts to promote cooperative economics are designed in essence to get people to think beyond the logic of capitalism. But we should be clear that running a food co-op or a cooperative buying club isn't the same thing as having state power where you can redistribute resources."[10] As Yakini suggests, while not having access to mechanisms of state power or control over capitalist markets, DBCFSN has sought to increase access to healthy and organically grown food for those who ordinarily would not be able to afford it, using alternative distribution strategies to build self-sufficiency.

While DBCFSN has only fifty registered members, those members have a significant voice on the national and international food justice scene. Its activities draw hundreds of tourists and regular volunteers. Most members are black women and lifelong residents of Detroit. Some are longtime activists and have deep backgrounds as gardeners, while others have never planted before. The organization's community outreach on food security and urban agriculture has helped build its membership. Its board of directors determines organizational policies and appoints the executive director, who handles daily operations.

DBCFSN members channel their energies into five substantive areas: the development of a citywide food policy, political and agricultural education, cooperative economics, marketing and farming, and using agriculture as a strategy to rebuild community. It has become a major influence in the national food justice movement and since 2006 has redirected the attention of organic and local food activists to issues of racial and economic inequality and food access. Because of DBCFSN's commitment to address and confront issues of race and class privilege, it has demanded a seat at the food justice table for African Americans and those who are food insecure. Until 2009, DBCFSN operated as a completely volunteer organization. That year, the network received funding from the W. W. Kellogg Foundation's Food and Community program for capacity building. Ever since, it has employed an office manager, farm manager, executive director, and education and outreach director. What follows is a description of the ways that DBCFSN enacts the basic principles of the CACR framework in its various projects, emphasizing the strategies of prefigurative politics, economic autonomy, and commons as praxis.

The Detroit Food Policy Council

In June 2006, Yakini and DBCFSN board president Mutope Al-Alkebulan attended a meeting of the city of Detroit's Neighborhood and Community Service Standing Committee, chaired by councilwoman JoAnne Watson. Yakini and Al-Alkebulan's presentation detailed the crisis of food access for the black community and the need for a policy to address the community's food needs. Watson asked the group to propose a policy that would address the needs they had outlined and that the city council could consider for a vote.

In order to develop a comprehensive food policy that incorporated feedback from Detroit residents and maintained a strong community focus, DBCFSN conducted listening sessions, community meetings, and a public review over the course of the following year. DBCFSN also studied food policies from other cities. Based on this, they recommended developing a food-system analysis for Detroit, collecting data on hunger and malnutrition, formulating recommendations for alternative community-based food systems such as urban agriculture, creating citizen and political education guidelines, and producing an emergency response plan in the event of a natural disaster. In March 2008, the city council unanimously approved the food-policy proposal and called for the establishment of the Detroit Food Policy Council to implement its mandates.

To represent all voices, DBCFSN proposed that the Detroit Food Policy Council match the city's demographic structure and that it be balanced in its composition of community members. To achieve this, it proposed twenty-one seats on the council. The city council and the mayor would each appoint one representative. The director of the Department of Health and Wellness Promotion or his or her designee would serve on the committee. Six seats were designated for grassroots community members, and the remaining seats would represent other sectors of the food system, including those involved in food production, distribution (retail and wholesale distributors), and consumption (including restaurants, schools, colleges and universities, and emergency food providers). Membership was limited to those who live or work in Detroit.

While city policies typically begin on the initiative of an elected official or other political entities, DBCFSN offered a food policy informed by the needs and desires of the community. Its members identified the lack of a policy and sought to create one using the principles of community building and community education. The written recommendations articulated the principles of fairness and equity for a hunger-free populace "that has access to fresh produce and other healthy food choices; a city in which the residents are educated about healthy food choices, and understand their relationship to the food system; a city in which urban agriculture and other sustainable practices contribute to its economic vitality; and a city in which all of its residents, workers, guests and visitors are treated with respect, justice and dignity by those from whom they obtain food."[11]

While the new food policy addressed city responses to food access, there were other factors that stood between Detroiters and healthy, affordable, organic food, including transportation and finances. In order to respond to residents' most immediate food needs, but also as a way to demonstrate the connection between agriculture and freedom, members of DBCFSN also began building an alternative food production system with particular emphasis on sustainable growing practices.

D-Town Farm

Yakini's experience as director of the Nsoroma Institute, an African-centered K-8 school that he cofounded in 1989, helped to inform the creation of D-Town Farm. *Nsoroma* means "children of the heavens" in the Twi language of Ghana. All teachers were required to incorporate concepts of food sovereignty and food security into the curriculum. Science classes included discussions about nutrition and soil health as well as lessons on food sovereignty and corporate control of the food system.

The school's garden was thoroughly integrated into its day-to-day activities, with faculty and staff maintaining it during school breaks. As parents and staff at the school became more interested in gardening and wanted to establish gardens in backyards and vacant lots, the Shamba Organic Gardening Collective was created. A team of "groundbreakers" helped those parents, staff, and community members till and prepare more than twenty gardens around the city. One of DBCFSN's founding goals was to establish a two-acre farm to produce food but also as a space to teach and show others how to become self-sufficient.

DBCFSN's first garden was created in 2006 on a quarter-acre plot of land on Detroit's east side near one of the only urban 4-H centers. After its first year, a developer bought the land and required DBCFSN to vacate the space. In 2007, DBCFSN moved to a half-acre parcel on the west side of Detroit owned by the Pan African Orthodox Christian Church. At that time, the organization began to use the name D-Town Farm. In March 2008, just before the start of the growing season, an official notified Yakini that the church had other plans for the land and D-Town Farm would have to relocate.

In May 2008, two years of negotiations with the city of Detroit for two acres of city-owned land came to fruition when officials asked DBCFSN to look at an unused location in the Meyers Tree Nursery in the city's Rouge Park. Yakini, Al-Alkebulan, and farm manager Marilyn Nefer Ra Barber viewed the site and agreed that it would work for D-Town Farm. In June 2008, with only a verbal agreement from the Recreation Department director, DBCFSN hired a black farmer from Belleville, Michigan, a rural town 29 miles southwest of Detroit, to till the area that was to become D-Town Farm's new home. By October of that year, DBCFSN attorneys and the city's attorneys had crafted a ten-year license agreement for the use of the two acres. In 2011, that agreement was amended to add an additional five acres.

A mother of the community helps a young girl prepare a potted plant at D-Town Farm in Detroit, August 2017. Photo by Jeremy Brockman.

Members of DBCFSN see the work of D-Town Farm as critical to their survival. They became involved in community farming for many reasons, including neighborhood beautification, ensuring Detroit residents' access to clean and healthy food, and becoming stewards of the environment. They engage in farming to reallocate land within the city for green purposes while meeting the needs of the local community. They also engage in farming as a community-based resistance strategy oriented toward political change. They hope that participating in the farm will plant seeds in the farmworkers' minds, demonstrating the critical nature of community-based control of collective resources.

Like members of the black southern farming cooperatives of the previous century, D-Town activists recognize farming as a strategy of resistance and sustainable community building. As Fannie Lou Hamer did before them, D-Town farmers have built new institutions on their own. They saw an opportunity to work toward food security/sovereignty and to gain greater control of the food system that affects their daily lives. Farming and food security became steps toward self-determination and self-reliance. When the community builds and controls its own social institutions, restoring the earth and transforming the food system become possible. D-Town farmers' resistance strategy focuses on their use of land to create community spaces, to teach about healthy eating, and to create a new vision of Detroit.

By the 2016 growing season, D-Town Farm was producing more than thirty different crops, including acorn squash, zucchini, kale, collard greens, tomatoes, basil, green beans, cabbage, watermelon, beets, turnips, radishes, and carrots, an unusually broad spectrum for a city farm. In addition to the fruit, vegetable, and herb crops, D-Town Farm was maintaining a mushroom-growing operation and an apiary that produced honey. D-Town also has hoop houses for year-round food production and runs a large-scale composting operation. Beyond these core agricultural activities, D-Town Farm serves as a community center and as a tangible example of collective work, self-reliance, and political agency. It is also a source, in accessible and inclusive language, of information about healthy food and healthy lifestyles rooted in African diasporic traditions. D-Town hosts an annual Harvest Festival that brings together hundreds of local, regional, and national supporters of the DBCFSN.

The Harvest Festival offers medical testing, such as screenings for high blood pressure and diabetes. In addition, a tour of the farm's medicinal herbs and workshops with nationally recognized chefs and registered nutritionists present opportunities for discussions about healthy cooking and the importance of nutrition and exercise. The Harvest Festival offers classes such as dance and yoga in a safe space and with a community. D-Town continually identifies ways to make wellness a community concern. Its project is a strategy of working with the earth while politicizing and mobilizing others around issues such as land and water use, access to healthy food, and conservation, pollution, and refuse management.

D-Town also hosts an annual agricultural internship program and manages the labor of regular volunteers. With funding from the Kellogg Foundation, DBCFSN has since 2010 employed farm managers who direct the work of staff and volunteers. A WHY Hunger grant has funded farm signage and tour-guide training to develop D-Town as a site for agri-tourism. The farm is a choice volunteer destination for hundreds of students from local and regional schools, as well as various community organizations.

D-Town produce is sold mainly at farmers' markets within the city, reflecting the farm's mission of feeding Detroiters. A few Detroit retail stores and restaurants are wholesale customers. The farm also has an on-site market stand on weekends. DBCFSN is a member organization of the Grown in Detroit (GID) cooperative, a collective of local youth, family, and community gardeners. GID is a part of Keep Growing Detroit, a movement with the mission of promoting Detroit as "a food sovereign city where the majority of fruits and vegetables Detroiters consume are grown by residents within the city's limits."[12] DBCFSN sets the price of its produce by averaging the current retail price for conventional and organic produce with the price that GID sets. Although not officially certified as organic, the produce is grown using sustainable practices.

DBCFSN's Prefigurative Politics

In its food policy development and in the creation and management of D-Town Farm, the DBCFSN has demonstrated a commitment to the democratic grassroots practices that characterize prefigurative politics. These community spaces allow for those who belong to oppressed groups to speak freely and to strategize as they transform conditions of oppression to conditions of self-sufficiency and self-determination. In both of these instances, the organization creates spaces and opportunities for community members to play a role in shaping the new programs and to participate in their governance. They have enacted Yakini's vision of political conversation as integral to community-based change and actively engage community members in crafting alternatives to the current food system.

While through the development of its food policy and subsequent food policy council DBCFSN petitioned the city government to increase residents' access to fresh food, D-Town farmers have demonstrated their agency by farming to feed themselves and their

An instructor teaches a class on meditation at D-Town Farm in Detroit, August 2017. Photo by Jeremy Brockman.

families. At the same time, they provide an example to their community of the benefits of hard work within a collective context and the joys of materially participating in producing healthy food for one's own table. Similar to Hamer's vision at Freedom Farm, at D-Town, food is a point of entry to discuss how African Americans might gain control over other aspects of their lives, including access to affordable housing, clean water, and decent public education. Through prefigurative politics, they create liberated spaces to first transform the minds of those around them and then to engage in actions that lead to their ability to control the kinds of food to which they have access.

D-Town farmers' work is a continuation of the civil rights and Black Power activism in which many of the organization's founding members were active. Their analysis of the food system identified race and class as barriers to accessing healthy and affordable food. In a time of convenience foods and easy access to unhealthy fast foods, "growing their own" has become a strategy of resistance but also a way of enacting an envisioned future. The food options created by D-Town Farm are but one way to work toward freedom and liberation for a community that has largely been left to its own devices to address the consequences of global and industrial economic catastrophe.

D-Town activists have created public space for the purposes of developing a healthy, well-fed, knowledgeable, and inspired African American community, but their efforts toward a sustainable community-based food system also foster a sense of self-determination and self-sufficiency for the community as a whole. Their participation in urban farming is part of their larger mission to end relationships of dependency and to educate the community about the importance of providing for themselves collectively. In response to the failure of the local government to provide a safe community and a range of social services, D-Town farmers have worked to build community and to place the earth at the center of their struggle for social transformation. Rather than investing their energy in opposing existing power structures through protest, they have chosen to develop a safe space through the transformation of their physical environment. In this way, the DBCFSN has imagined creative responses to community deprivation and political exclusion. The focus on developing institutions, a grassroots food system, and the environmental and policy infrastructure needed for an empowered self-sufficiency is helping them to create the foundations for a new world marked by new ways of being through D-Town.

DBCFSN's Promotion of Economic Autonomy

D-Town farmers describe the farm as a way to enhance their economic autonomy as well. Aba, a founding member of DBCFSN, directly relates her involvement in D-Town to the feeling of being abandoned by grocery retailers: "Particularly in Detroit, our grocery stores have been woefully inadequate in terms of clean [organic] food. The major grocery store chains have all left our city, and a lot of people felt very abandoned and almost helpless."[13] Linda also describes the lack of access to food as her reason for becoming involved in urban gardening: "There are no markets in our area;

therefore, people are not able to shop in their immediate area for healthy food, for fresh vegetables—as opposed to the canned foods and fast food that are the primary source of nutrition."[14] She began working at D-Town in order to obtain fresh vegetables for her family. D-Town farmers recognize that race and class influence their access to healthy foods. They have experienced neighborhood markets that are unkempt and stocked with foods past their expiration dates, as well as foodstuffs that show visible signs of mold and decay. They note that stores in white, affluent communities do not try to sell spoiled foods. Marilyn Nefer Ra, founder and the organization's first farm manager, points out that those who live in wealthy, predominantly white neighborhoods have the financial means to choose between conventional versus organically grown fruits and vegetables: "In the suburbs, there's a fruit market on every other corner."[15] She notes the importance of location in determining food security. Kwamenah, another organizational founder agrees: "Whites have better access to fruits and veggies in their own neighborhood. People in the suburbs make the choice to engage in urban farming. For D-Town farmers, it's a necessity."[16]

Many residents in Detroit are food insecure, which means that many of its citizens are forced to obtain a considerable portion of their food from "fringe" food retailers. Many of these stores specialize in the sale of alcohol, tobacco, and lottery tickets. They have a small selection of prepackaged and canned food products high in salt, fat, and sugar. As Kwamenah says, "The only access to food in Detroit is through party stores [using the Michigan term for liquor stores, which sell alcohol, tobacco, lottery tickets and prepared liquor and junk food] or gas stations or grocery stores that have inferior quality fruits and veggies, meat and poultry that is outdated, and they don't care about switching the labels to continue selling them."[17]

In 2007, Farmer Jack closed its doors on the residents of Detroit, leaving the entire city without a major chain grocery store.[18] Detroiters who had been able to patronize five major chain grocery stores within the city limits just a generation ago had none for five years, until a Whole Foods opened in 2012.[19] Both because of location and price, Whole Foods cannot adequately serve the entire city.

Thus, D-Town Farm as a source of food fills an urgent need. Black grassroots activists decided not to pin their hopes on, wait for, or expend their energy attempting to attract a supermarket to the city. Instead, by creating D-Town and laboring to ensure its stability even after being moved from two land sites, DBCFSN has taken control of the growing practices that precede members' food's arrival on their plates. Yet community members envision more than addressing their daily need for food: they are working to build knowledge about the soil and self-sufficient food ways—how to grow food and promote community independence—while also taking back economic opportunities associated with the harvest and distribution of food for the African American community.

Through farming, D-Town members argue, they can produce their own food, while investing in their communities and assisting community members to learn much-needed survival skills. Aba describes her participation in gardening as a way to develop self-determination and empowerment:

> Community gardening lets you decide the kinds of food you want to eat and grow, and the Detroit Black Community Food Security Network lets you have some input as to what is grown. You get to help in the entire process of growing the food. That addresses the problem of self-reliance. . . . I feel more by growing my own. I have experienced not having it, and I felt powerless. [Grocery stores] can come and go. . . . If I grow it myself, I know what's going to happen. I get more peace of mind knowing that I can grow it, freeze it, dry it. Even if there were a grocery store that consistently provided fresh produce in my neighborhood, I would still participate [at D-Town] because I need to be able to control it myself.[20]

Others agree that community gardening promotes a general sense of self-determination. Ebony, another founder, says, "The reason I'm engaged in farming is self-determination. It is important for us to create for ourselves and define our own realities, and the reasons that we should be doing anything when it comes to businesses, housing, anything, we should be in control of that. Being in Detroit, a predominantly black city, it's important for us to determine, for those of us who know, to be in control of the food system in Detroit because there are a lot of us who don't know."[21] Ebony also considers the gardens essential to survival when she describes what can happen when citizens rely on others to meet their needs: "The reality [is] that at any moment on any given day, the folks who control the grocery stores can say, 'You know what? We tired of y'all. We are going to make our money somewhere else, or we are not going to sell what you want us to sell.' You need to be able to feed yourself rather than waiting, you need to know how to grow it yourself instead of waiting on somebody down the street to sell it to you or choose not to."[22] Malik extends the argument that community gardening is a means to gain control of the community: "I've been involved in efforts to build greater degrees of self-sufficiency or self-reliance in the black community and control of our communities. A logical extension of that work is to grasp larger control over the food system as it impacts us in our communities. That, in turn, led to gardening."[23] Aba similarly sees gardening as a way to gain control of her life and her community in general: "I heard that if you control the food supply, you can control the people; you don't need guns, you don't need bombs. To control what my children eat is very important to me. Community gardening is very political because it puts control in my hands. We won't have to live from someone else's hands, and neither will my children when they learn how to grow their own food."[24]

Farming and gardening are far more than the production of food. As Malik says, "It isn't just an issue of having access to fresh produce in the community. It's also an issue of who controls that fresh produce and who profits from the sale of it. So even if there are stores selling fresh produce, we still benefit from building as high a degree of self-reliance as we can."[25] Similarly, Ebony mentions her own involvement as a continuation of the legacy of those who were enslaved and who brought over agricultural traditions and seeds. She says, "Resistance started before enslavement ended. When our ancestors were kidnapped and brought over here, they stowed seeds that were native to their land, that we now know were native to the areas that they were taken from. These foods are staples in our diet. . . . They were holding on to their culture. They were holding on to home. That right there is resistance."[26] Similarly, Tee suggests that her involvement is an undeniable, everyday act of resistance: "Gardening in the city of Detroit is saying, 'Fuck it!' It says, 'I can grow my own food, and I can feed my community.' You are dealing with a majority [African American] population that has been scarred, battered, and bruised. The first step to rebuilding a culture is agriculture."[27] In making these kinds of statements, D-Town farmers echo Fannie Lou Hamer when she said, "Down in Mississippi they are killing Negroes of all ages, on the installment plan, through starvation."[28] By controlling their food, D-Town farmers enact a strategy of resistance that has been vital to African Americans for generations.

DBCFSN's vision of freedom began with food production, but it led to the building of alternative economic institutions. Based on their experiences, its members believed that controlling food access could move Detroit residents from a state of dependence upon others, who often provided substandard food, and toward economic autonomy.[29] Traditional grocery stores operate according to what might be considered a resource extraction model. Major chain grocery stores receive their profits from neighborhoods where the shareholders do not live and where they often have no other investments; the proceeds go to storeowners, stakeholders, and investment brokers who have no specific vested interest in community development. Cooperatives owned by communities are an alternative to resource extraction; they represent a resource generation model that is critical to progressive community development.

Early on, DBCFSN identified the goal of a community-owned food cooperative as a way to provide residents with healthy foodstuffs, nutritional supplements, and sustainable household products, and to teach the principles of collective work and cooperative economics. The organization started the Ujamaa Food Buying Club in 2008. *Ujamaa* is the Kiswahili word for "collective economics." The buying club allows members to aggregate their buying power to make purchases from a food distributor who delivers their orders to the DBCFSN office at a reduced cost. Co-op membership is broader than the general membership of DBCFSN and more racially diverse. The coop provides Detroiters an opportunity to save money, nourish their bodies, and pool their economic resources. The co-op has operated continuously and successfully for almost nine years, using many of the same strategies sharecroppers and tenant farmers used in Freedom Farm Cooperative. As of 2018, DBCFSN was close to beginning construction of the Detroit Food Commons, a major development to be located in Detroit's North End, the anchor of which will be the Detroit People's Food Co-op, a full-service cooperatively owned grocery store. Funded by grants, donations, and federally subsidized loans, the Detroit Food Commons will also house a healthy-foods restaurant, an incubator kitchen, a community meeting space, and the offices of DBCFSN.

DBCFSN: Building Commons as Praxis

While participants began D-Town Farm as an effort to control and secure their food supply, the farm came to have much broader significance as a location to practice the principles of cooperatives and social responsibility. The farmers chose to take responsibility for securing their own access to fresh fruits and vegetables, to develop vacant land through their own self-reliance and agency, and to enact these qualities in multiple areas of their lives. While individual families have grown food in Detroit in their backyard gardens for as long as there have been city residents, D-Town Farm represented an opportunity to demonstrate social responsibility by contributing to the provision of food as community wellness. Like Freedom Farm Cooperative before them, D-Town represents the enactment of commons as praxis by showing the political possibilities inherent in collective work. The farm offers and illustrates a new vision for the city at a time when many of its residents have given up hope.

As Aba suggests, D-Town is a public example. Many Detroit residents are transforming city land into spaces that produce food, showcase public art, and inspire those who witness it. She says, "The farm is a light. . . . [It] helps people see what can be done with nothing. . . . Look at what we have done on vacant land with nothing."[30]

The need has never been more urgent. Well before the city of Detroit filed for bankruptcy in 2013, many community health and social programs were cut and community centers closed, eliminating crucial supports and activities in the city and most directly affecting the community's vulnerable residents: children and senior citizens. D-Town's services address this gap, providing centers where people learn about healthy eating, access healthy food, receive health services, and participate in physical activity.

D-Town Farm has also created employment opportunities for young people. Kwamenah is both a former employee of the city and one of DBCFSN's founding members. He says he got involved in D-Town because the closing of recreation centers left him concerned that children would have nothing to do in the summer. He was also interested in growing healthy, organic produce and providing it to those who would not otherwise be able to afford it.[31] Aba describes D-Town as a center of activity. The center provides opportunities for different generations to engage collaboratively in positive, productive projects. She says, "Everyone takes part, and everyone seems to have a stake in its success. It gives everyone in the community something to do . . . the children, elders. . . . You gain a great sense of satisfaction seeing something go from a seed to your table."[32] Malik argues that farming "builds community; it builds a sense of cohesion and collective action; it builds intergenerational dialogue and intergenerational work. Many times folks involved in gardening are older people . . . and giving older people a chance to work with younger generations and pass on that knowledge is important."[33]

Typically, education about healthy food choices and exercise begins in elementary school, where many children first encounter the food pyramid, now known as the food plate.[34] After that initial exposure, most learning regarding healthy lifestyles comes from such sources as social media, news reports, academic studies, websites, public service announcements, fitness clubs, and health-food establishments. Low-income African Americans do not have ready access to many of these informational sources. Moreover, many people have difficulty reading and interpreting the information on the nutrition labels printed on packaged foods. As Russell

DBCFSN's Food Warriors program at the Shrine of the Black Madonna in Detroit, July 2017. Photo by Jeremy Brockman.

Rothman and colleagues have shown, education, literacy, and income influence comprehension of food labels, and the interpretation of the nutritional information on packaged food to which wealthier people have access supports healthier choices.[35] Members of D-Town use the farm as an accessible source of food information and assume the role of information disseminators about nutrition in their communities. D-Town farmers deliver information about the importance of food choices, the dangers of unhealthy food, and the benefits of exercise within culturally relevant and easily accessible formats directed specifically at the African American community, such as through community workshops and church events.

Ebony, another DBCFSN founder who as an educator worked with Yakini at Nsoroma, uses her work on the farm as the context within which she provides information about her healthy, vegetarian diet to others in her community. She says,

Because of my own diet, the choices that I make personally—I am vegetarian and trying to eat organic and those kinds of things—I wanted to be able to reach people outside myself who are new to eating healthy or haven't been exposed yet to it. So by being involved in community gardening, it gives us an opportunity to open up other African Americans' eyes to the importance of food. . . . We take food for granted. . . . Even those who are struggling, we don't have the appreciation for food. If we knew how important food was, I just don't think we would make the choices that we do.[36]

D-Town farmers offer workshops and training sessions at the farm. These include cooking and raw-food-preparation demonstrations using culturally significant ingredients, such as collard greens, okra, black-eyed peas, and other plants that traveled through the Middle Passage. At the request of community organizations and church groups, they go off-site to give presentations about healthy food choices. The organization's members also volunteer their time during the Harvest Festival to lead discussions and give presentations about composting, beekeeping, growing food in small spaces, and the importance of sustainable agriculture. At such events, D-Town farmers speak from an explicitly African American perspective to inform citizens about healthy lifestyles such as veganism, vegetarianism, and preparing and eating raw foods. Marilyn Nefer Ra suggests that the D-Town farmers have been successful because they have "raised the awareness of the need for healthier foods and the fact that Detroit is a food desert."[37]

Kwamenah connects gardening with the scarcity of conventional medical care in Detroit: "We don't seem to have access to medical care that other communities have on an ongoing basis due to employment status. . . . We need to learn how to go back to basics of what our parents did down South—cook food locally, cook nutritiously, understand why our parents lived into their eighties and nineties."[38]

Encouraging those who attend their events to engage in food production is a way to spread the word that Detroiters can regain control of the food choices in their community. By raising awareness of the hazards of manufactured foods, D-Town calls attention to the importance of this effort and connects its work to African Americans over centuries who used food production as a strategy toward freedom. When community members control the production of their food, assess its quality, and distribute that information to others, healthier food reaches the community. This is the guiding principle of DBCFSN and typifies the relationships it nurtures.

From Decay into Compost

The work of the members of the Detroit Black Community Food Security Network provides another vivid example of how communities have used strategies of collective agency and community resilience to produce and distribute food for self-determination, self-sufficiency, community building, and wellness. Engaging agriculture to rebuild community yields increased access to healthy, affordable food options for city residents and opportunities that move toward economic autonomy and independence. Not only do these efforts illustrate the strategies of collective agency and community resilience, but they harken back to earlier historical moments when African Americans turned to agriculture as a way to feed themselves, share resources, build community, and work toward freedom and liberation. The work of members of DBCFSN to create a food policy and a policy council and to establish D-Town Farm and the Detroit People's Coop illustrates the value of working toward self-sufficiency and self-determination through the development of community-based food systems. As the breakfast programs of the Black Panther Party and the Freedom Farm Cooperative demonstrated in their times, DBCFSN's focus on community wellness is a critical starting point that shows how by providing food for the community, solutions to problems in politics, education, housing, and policing become more possible.

Given Detroit's historic economic collapse, some have called for the city's figurative autopsy.[39] In much the same way that Detroiters' labor, innovation, and creativity put the world on wheels, the current urban agriculture movement offers the rest of the nation lessons on building healthy communities and community wellness, using food as its base. Members of DBCFSN and their allies have decided that instead of giving the city's eulogy, they will turn decay into compost, building on what remains from the earlier iteration of the city by transforming available land, vacant lots, and ingenuity into gardens full of music, food, art, education, and celebration of the future. While many of these changes could have been made under local government initiative, they were not. What makes these changes significant is that those who chose to stay in the city are creating the neighborhoods and the spaces they need, mostly independently of local government. Detroit's urban agricultural movement leads the nation, tapping into the city's rich history of innovation. The DBCFSN's model invites us to think differently about cities, about food, about local food, about the economics of healthy food, and about justice. Those who have lived in and loved the city for generations recognize, through DCBSFN and its affiliated organizations, that its model can once again lead the nation.

Black Farmers and Black Land Matter

> Collective black self-recovery takes place when we begin to renew
> our relationship to the earth, when we remember the way of our
> ancestors . . . Living in modern society without history, it has been easy
> to forget that black people were first and foremost people of the land,
> farmers. —bell hooks

This powerful statement by bell hooks refers to the reclamation of a historical legacy. It links that reclamation to collective black self-recovery, which is so important given the economic calamity African American communities are experiencing today.

We tend to be more familiar with the history of slavery, sharecropping, and tenant farming and the exploitation and oppression agriculture involved. That history is full of pain, trauma, exploitation, and even death. But the blossoming and expansion of the current African American urban agricultural movement encourages us to dig deeper, ask another set of questions, and, therefore, expand what we thought we knew about black people's relationship to the land.

Freedom Farmers charts a new narrative. It asks the question, If pain was all there was, how can we explain the indigenous roots of the current urban farming movement—spearheaded by black people? If pain was all there was, why should black people voluntarily return to a form of work that produced exploitation and oppression— so much so that it forced people to flee from the South? *Freedom Farmers* provides answers to those questions and more by pursuing another aspect of the history—one that uncovers black people's complex relationship to the land—as a way to understand, share, and ultimately write a different kind of narrative.

Freedom Farmers has shown how popularly assumed understandings that singularly view farming and agriculture as simply an oppressive yoke around the neck of black people are incomplete, narrow, and (even worse) debilitating in their power to erase a legacy of horticultural knowledge, a rich expression of struggle, a foundation for building institutions, and the potential for learning lessons borne of collective struggle. Grappling with the travails and how they gave rise to black farmers' responses provides an enriched story and a counternarrative that unveils the way that black people not only have been connected to the land but have used the land individually and collectively to challenge white supremacy and political and economic exploitation. Indeed, *Freedom Farmers* turns overlooked and forgotten scraps of history into nutrient-rich historical compost, revealing multiple narratives of resistance that illustrate how and in what ways land has mattered to black people's struggles against marginalization for independence.

This work builds on scholarship about the importance of agriculture for African American communities in the civil rights movement.[1] For instance, Spencer Wood's work captures the story of the farmers in Mississippi who welcomed and organized the work of the Freedom Riders—students who traveled from the North to participate in civil rights struggles—and who supported other activists fighting for the right to vote and to integrate public institutions. Others discuss the role and importance of black landowners as farmers. This is an important corrective because while much has been written about the Freedom Riders, far less has been written about the black farmers who welcomed, supported, fed, and even used their land to bail activists out of jail for their political participation.

Black farmers mattered. They were not passive victims. They acted, not only to improve their own and their communities' circumstances but to advance a broader political and activist agenda to challenge racially oppressive rural social structures. Their labor on and off the farm, and through the leveraging of their land resources, provided crucial support for activists working for change in other arenas, such as voting rights and the fight against segregation.

Yet the literature is biased toward urban narratives of struggle and tends to overlook farming and black working-class farmers. It focuses on more obvious strategies of resistance, such as protest marches and boycotts, while ignoring the realities of the majority of those who were living in the South. It emphasizes the privileges of landowners while ignoring the realities of the overwhelming majority of farmers and the ways that they resisted. Excluding black farmers and others like them from the historical account has made a group of signally important actors in the struggle—namely, farmers—seem passive or distant from the black freedom struggle. As a result, the histories of African Americans and agriculture do not inspire communities to reconnect with that heritage.

Contrary to popular perceptions, African Americans fought for their right to own and control land, grow food, and maintain their livelihoods and identities as farmers. *Freedom Farmers* challenges the assumption that black people simply did not want to farm and that it was this desire to escape hard work and their negative relationship to the land that caused African Americans to migrate to the North. The truth was more complicated than that; while the exploitative relationships under which black farmers labored shaped and mediated their relationship to the land, their work, their safety, and their ability to survive and thrive in those places, the land was still the place where they lived, worked, and constructed family and community.

By recuperating the early nineteenth-century approaches and legacies to food, farming, and land—Booker T. Washington's ideas about how to build institutions to support community-based agriculture, George Washington Carver's systematic scientific contributions to an organic and sustainable agricultural practice, and W. E. B. Du Bois's insights into the political power of cooperatives—*Freedom Farmers* documents the crucial contributions of agriculture to black community development and struggles for independence. Growing food was a life-affirming, collective strategy. Liberatory agriculture ignited the imagination of farmer-activists in African-American farming cooperatives during the mid-twentieth century. In the twenty-first century, self-determined agriculture alongside the lessons learned from decades of successes and failures have the real potential to offer a similar opportunity for urban growers who are responding to the harsh conditions of deindustrialization and economic downturn.

Drawing on three examples from the 1960s and 1970s, *Freedom Farmers* illustrates the agency of those who stayed on the land and supported black freedom struggles, including their own. These often impoverished farmers shifted from cash crops to food crops as a way to build community. As they worked to build sustainable communities, they simultaneously challenged the exploitative relationships of the southern food system through cooperative agriculture at various scales.

Fannie Lou Hamer's Freedom Farm Cooperative offers an example of what could happen when folks who were largely unemployed, and in many cases lacked even the basic necessities to live, pooled their resources to build a cooperative agricultural community. Through the North Bolivar County Farmers Cooperative, the type of work employed by Freedom Farm operated at a countywide level, with a movement committed to assisting member cooperatives and building mechanisms that would lift people out of poverty. On an even larger scale, the Federation of Southern Cooperatives provided support for cooperatives across the South. Examining FFC and NBCFC alongside FSC exposes some of the limits of local and countywide organizations, such as the greater challenges these smaller organizations face in accessing support from external sources, leveraging economies of scale, and developing wide pools of expertise. While grassroots cooperatives like FFC and NBCFC represent the locations where economic autonomy, commons as praxis, and prefigurative politics are built and acted out, FSC, also black-led and run, provided essential resources for their projects. Drawing expertise and talent from all over the country, FSC's support of the local and countywide efforts created firm foundations on all levels by offering the educational resources and information on best practices in everything from agriculture techniques to bookkeeping, from preparing for tax audits to achieving broadly defined community development goals. FSC's vision was all-inclusive, eventually providing support in all of the areas that a cooperative might need: health care, education, food and nutrition, overall wellness, community centers, senior centers, and housing. As an umbrella organization, its goal was not to solve a cooperative's problems; rather, once a community defined a problem, FSC would provide the resources to solve it in a way that was cooperative and community-based.

Collective agency and community resilience are essential building blocks. They undergird the ideas of Washington, Carver, Du Bois, and Hamer, and the creative practices of the cooperatives. They are strategies that have to be understood within a particular social context. Resilience is a response to a catastrophic event. With it, a community is capable of putting itself back together. The concept, which has tended to focus on individual people and therefore individualized success and failure, has been criticized for not interrogating or pushing back against the structural factors that may have caused the catastrophic event in the first place. But the notion of collective resilience demonstrated by "Freedom Farmers" is qualitatively different. It is not about an individual responding to crisis, but an intentional, organized collective response. While not uniformly successful, through cooperatives, the community response to crises was one that engaged in reflection on structures of power.

When black farmers in the South in the 1960s tried to vote and were not allowed to—and were evicted from their plots of land for making the attempt—the collective helped them to respond to that crisis in a way that was profoundly political. In this sense, community resilience is a way for a community to absorb a disturbance and to reorganize itself while undergoing change. While resilience as a concept often doesn't emphasize structural factors, *community* resilience does take into account structural approaches and community engagement that includes indigenous knowledge and emotional experiences, and the kind of interracial and intraracial exchanges that we need to adapt.

In my study of the cooperatives, three strategies emerged as elements of collective agency and community resilience and as factors crucial to their success: commons as praxis, prefigurative politics, and economic autonomy. Commons as praxis was evident in the ways these cooperatives shared resources, ideas, labor, and solutions in order to respond to institutional racism and the conditions of poverty. It was visible in the collective institutions they crafted to circumvent the hostile and unequal institutions they faced in the wider world. The cases examined here show the importance of circulation of ideas between experts (such as George Washington Carver, Booker T. Washington and W. E. B. Du Bois) and practitioners (Fannie Lou Hamer) who work the land, and the importance of democratic and collective discussion of those ideas.

Similarly, in a time when African Americans were not allowed to vote and were not allowed to have a voice, prefigurative politics were crucial. Even in conditions where they were denied the right to participate in electoral politics, within these cooperatives they were allowed to contribute to the direction of their organizations. It was one-person one-vote, and the cooperative members acted as if they were full citizens. Engaging in prefigurative politics within these cooperatives provided a taste of freedom and allowed them to embody freedom, justice, and equity within their institutions. The cases illustrate the importance of political education in building the capacity of grassroots communities to pursue strategies that lead toward freedom.

Similarly, economic autonomy was critical to the cooperatives' success. A community that relies upon someone else for its well-being feels beholden. The cooperatives in this study began to visualize what it would look like to be financially and politically free and to have all that they needed. Developing economic autonomy required them to decide what was in their best interest and consider how to achieve it. The cases of FFC and NBCFC showed how grassroots collectives gained access to the resources they needed to begin to produce in ways that were independent of an exploitative and racially oppressive local social structure. The case of FSC revealed how local cooperatives can benefit from being part of networks that provide technical and logistical support and that work toward development of alternative regional food systems.

These three strategies are the building blocks of collective agency and community resilience. They were the necessary tools that groups employed to begin to grasp what freedom feels like.

Through protests, marches, and boycotts, we can speak out against oppression and exploitation, against what we don't like or what holds us hostage or oppresses us. Strategies of collective agency and community resilience turn that energy and attention toward building what looks like freedom politically and economically in an inclusive way.

Freedom Farmers excavates the history of more than a century of African American farmers whose labor, on the land and in community, has been ignored. But it also looks forward, for it aims to offer context, support, and suggestions to urban food activists like those in Detroit, who are involved in redesigning what their city, with agriculture at its base, could look like. In many ways, these twenty-first-century urban agricultural movements are already implementing the elements of collective agency and community resilience: making community decisions, creating democratic and inclusive organizational structures, and building new infrastructures that lead to economic autonomy. Hopefully this book will provide them with further inspiration and ideas for this crucial, challenging, and liberatory work.

Notes

INTRODUCTION

1. See Balvanz et al., "Next Generation"; Daniel, *Dispossession*; Demissie, "History of Black Farm Operators"; Gilbert and Eli, *Homecoming*; Gilbert, Sharp, and Felin, "Loss and Persistence of Black-Owned Farms"; Hurt, *African American Life*; Pennick, "Struggle for Control of America's Production Agriculture System"; Pierre-Louis, "Farmers and Land Loss"; and Reid, "African Americans and Land Loss in Texas."

2. See Wood, *Roots of Black Power*.

3. This work builds upon the scholarship on black farmers' organizations and the resistance strategies they have engaged in efforts to obtain civil and human rights. For additional information, see de Jong, "With the Aid of God and the F.S.A."; de Jong, *Different Day*; Gray, *History of Agriculture in the Southern United States*; Johnson, *Shadow of the Plantation*; Mandle, "Roots of Black Poverty"; Marshall and Godwin, *Cooperatives and Rural Poverty in the South*; McGee and Boone, *Black Rural Landowner*; Perlo, *Negro in Southern Agriculture*; Raper, *Preface to Peasantry*; Raper, *Tenants of the Almighty*; Reid, *Reaping a Greater Harvest*; and Woofter, *Black Yeomanry*.

4. For scholarship on African American migration, see Leman, *Promised Land*; Painter, *Exodusters*; and Hahn, *Nation under Our Feet*.

5. See White, "Sisters of the Soil"; White, "Shouldering Responsibility for the Delivery of Human Rights"; and White, "D-Town Farm."

6. Scott and Kerkvliet, *Everyday Forms of Peasant Resistance*, 108.

7. Some works that suggest such a pathway is possible are Kelley, *Hammer and Hoe*; Hunter, *To Joy My Freedom*; Haley, *No Mercy Here*; and LeFlouria, *Chained in Silence*.

8. See Glaser and Holton, "Remodeling Grounded Theory."

9. See Walker and Salt, *Resilience Thinking*; and Ann S. Masten, "Resilience in Developing Systems."

10. See Cooper, "Intersectional Travel through Everyday Utopias."

11. See Escobar and Harcourt, "Practices of Difference."

12. See Futrell and Simi, "Free Spaces, Collective Identity, and the Persistence of U.S. White Power Activism." See also Polletta, "'Free Spaces' in Collective Action."

13. See Evans and Boyte, *Free Spaces*; Rao and Dutta, "Free Spaces as Organizational Weapons of the Weak"; and Groch, "Free Spaces."

14. Carney and Rosomoff, *In the Shadow of Slavery*, 122.

15. Carney and Rosomoff, 105. See also Joyner, *Down by the Riverside*.

16. See Carney, "With Grains in Her Hair."

17. Carney and Rosomoff, *In the Shadow of Slavery*, 112.

18. Carney and Rosomoff, 121.

19. See Barickman, "Bit of Land, Which They Call Roça."

20. See Tomich, *Slavery in the Circuit of Sugar*.

21. Barickman, "Bit of Land, Which They Call Roça," 649.

22. See Mintz, *Tasting Food, Tasting Freedom*.

23. See Cha-Jua, *America's First Black Town*; Sitton, Conrad, and Orton, *Freedom Colonies*; and Painter, *Exodusters*.

24. See Douglas Blackmon, *Slavery by Another Name*. See Denby, *Indignant Heart*, for a narrative on displaced black farm communities in Lowndes County, Alabama, by plantation owners during the Selma-to-Montgomery march. Denby, a black militant from Detroit, got black autoworkers to raise money to buy land for displaced black farm families in Lowndes County and organized an event for Martin Luther King Jr. at Cobo Arena to raise support and resources for black farmers in Lowndes County.

25. See Dann, "Black Populism"; and Millar, "Black Protest and White Leadership."

26. These candidates were often affiliated with the national Republican Party, which retained status as the traditional party of black voters through the late 1960s. Cooperatives also advanced and supported third-party candidates.

27. Ali, *In the Lion's Mouth*, 71.

28. See Cronon, *Black Moses*.

29. Hill, *Marcus Garvey and Universal Negro Improvement Association Papers*, Vol. 1: 1826–1919, 128.

30. Hill, 178. See also: *Populism in the South Revisited: New Interpretations and New Departures*, ed. James M. Beeby. University of Mississippi Press with essay on agrarianism and garveyism.

31. "Introduction: Reframing Global Justice," in: Mullings L. (ed) *New Social Movements in the African Diaspora*. The Critical Black Studies Series (Institute for Research in African American Studies), Palgrave Macmillan, New York, 2009.

32. Hill, *Marcus Garvey and Universal Negro Improvement Association Papers*, 7: 957–58. See also Mantler, *Power to the Poor Black-Brown Coalition*.

33. See McKnight, *Last Crusade*. See also Jones, *March on Washington*; Garrow, *Bearing the Cross*; Branch, *Parting the Waters*; and Jackson, *From Civil Rights to Human Rights*.

34. Quoted in Dyson, *I May Not Get There with You*, 12.

35. Quoted in Pohlmann, *Confrontation vs. Compromise*, 9.

36. See Abron, "Serving the People"; Kirkby, "Revolution Will Not Be Televised"; Patel, "Survival Pending Revolution"; and Potori, "Feeding Revolution."

37. Alkebulan, *Survival Pending Revolution*, 32.

38. Alkebulan, 35. See also Nelson, *Body and Soul*.

39. Quoted in Marable and Mullings, *Let Nobody Turn Us Around*, 450.

40. Rashid Nuri, farm manager for the Nation of Islam, personal communication, March 2015.

41. See McCutcheon, "Community Food Security 'For Us, by Us'"; and McCutcheon, "Returning Home to Our Rightful Place."

42. See White, "D-Town Farm"; and White, "Sisters of the Soil."

43. Members of DBCFSN use *Mama* and *Baba*, Swahili terms of endearment and respect.

44. See Gray, "Community Land Trusts in the United States."

45. Wendell Paris, personal communication, October, 2013.

46. See Anderson, *Emmett Till*.

CHAPTER 1

1. See Reynolds, *Black Farmers in America*.

2. See Reid and Bennett, *Beyond Forty Acres and a Mule*.

3. Washington, *Working with the Hands*, 135.

4. Washington, "Industrial Education for the Negro," 9–10.

5. See Moore, *Booker T. Washington*. See also Norrell, *Up from History*; and Smock, *Booker T. Washington*.

6. Washington, "Industrial Education for the Negro," 9–10.

7. Washington, *Up from Slavery*, 136.

8. See Tullos, "Black Belt."

9. Washington, "Southern Letter XVI," 3.

10. Woodson and Logan, "Negro in Education," 13.

11. Washington, "Farmer's College on Wheels," 8352. See also Mayberry, *Role of Tuskegee University*, 7.

12. Washington, "Industrial Education for the Negro," 10.

13. These thirty-three trades were as follows: carpentry, blacksmithing, printing, wheelwrighting, harness making, painting, machinery, founding, shoemaking, brick masonry, brickmaking, plastering, sawmilling, tinsmithing, tailoring, mechanical drawing, architectural drawing, electrical engineering, steam engineering, canning, sewing, dressmaking, millinery, cooking, laundering, housekeeping, mattress making, basketry, nursing,

agriculture, dairying, stock raising, and horticulture. Hammond Lamont, "Character Building at Tuskegee," in Lamont, *Negro Self-Help*, 20.

14. Washington, "Industrial Education for the Negro," 21.

15. See Jones, "Role of Tuskegee Institute."

16. Washington, "Twenty-five Years of Tuskegee," 8352.

17. Meier, "Booker T. Washington and the Town of Mound Bayou," 339–40.

18. *Tuskegee Student*, December 2, 1897.

19. An exhaustive list is impossible to compile, but schools that credited their founding to one or more Tuskegee graduates included Voorhees Industrial School, Denmark, S.C.; Topeka Normal Institute in Topeka, Kan. Port Royal Agricultural School in Beaufort, S.C.; Mt. Meigs Colored Institute (founded 1889) in Waugh, Ala.; Hawkinsville Rural and Industrial School (founded 1899) in Hawkinsville, Ala.; Jacksonian Enterprise School (founded 1893) in Newville, Ala.; William J. Edwards' Snow Hill Normal and Industrial Institute in Snow Hill, Ala.; Colored Union Literary and Industrial School in China, Ala.; Voorhees Industrial School (founded 1897) in Denmark, S.C.; Robert Hungerford Industrial School (founded 1899) in Eatonville, Fla.; Centerville Industrial Institute (founded 1900) in Centerville, Ala.; Charity Industrial School (founded 1906) in Lowndes County, Ala.; Utica Normal and Industrial Institute (founded 1903) in Utica, Miss.; North Louisiana Agricultural and Industrial Institute (founded 1908) now known as Grambling State University located in Grambling, Louisiana, Cordova Institute (founded 1902) in Cordova, S.C.; Haloche Industrial Institute (founded 1903) Taft, OK; Mary H. Holliday Public School in Yellow Bayou Plantation, Luna Landing, Ark.; and Piney Woods Country Life High School located in Piney Woods, MS, a boarding school for African American youth).

20. See Harrison, *Piney Woods School*.

21. Jones, "Role of Tuskegee Institute," 255.

22. *Montgomery Advertiser*, February 24, 1892.

23. Lamont, *Negro Self-Help*, 8.

24. Jones, 261.

25. See Washington, "Southern Letter XVI."

26. See Richardson, "Negro Farmers of Alabama." See also Scott, *Reluctant Farmer*, 233. Not only was Campbell the first African American agent, but Tuskegee Institute was in reality the first college to cooperate directly in Seaman Knapp, considered the founder of agricultural education and extension program.

27. Richardson, "Negro Farmers of Alabama."

28. Richardson, 384. See also R. Scott, *Reluctant Farmer*.

29. Jones, "Education of Black Farmers," 265.

30. Jones, 40.

31. See Ferguson, "Caught in 'No Man's Land.'"

32. Mary Simpson, farmer, quoted in Campbell, *Movable School Goes to the Negro Farmer*, 139.

33. Jones, "Role of Tuskegee Institute," 267.

34. Parks's parents were farmers and may well have received some benefit from Tuskegee.

35. See Jones, "Role of Tuskegee Institute."

36. "The Farming Problem in the Black Belt," *Southern Workman* 30 (1901): 189. See also Washington, "Winners from the Soil."

37. Hersey and Sutter, *My Work Is That of Conservation*, 46.

38. Kremer, *George Washington Carver: A Biography*, 7.

39. See Finlay, "Old Efforts at New Uses."

40. See, for example, Federer, *George Washington Carver*; Kremer, *George Washington Carver: A Biography*; and Vella, *George Washington Carver*.

41. An exception is Hersey and Sutter, *My Work Is That of Conservation*.

42. See Hersey and Sutter. According to the George Washington Carver National Monument Committee, Carver was born in 1864. As with many African Americans who were born during slavery, the exact date of his birth is not known, and there is no record.

43. Kremer, *George Washington Carver: A Biography*, 20.

44. Kremer, 20.

45. Kremer, 4.

46. Kremer, 6.

47. See Kremer, *George Washington Carver: In His Own Words*.

48. George Washington Carver Papers at Tuskegee Institute, microfilm, series 2: "Correspondence, 1896–99," frames 0754–73, reel 1, 81–82, Wisconsin Historical Society Archives, Madison, accessed October 2015.

49. "Correspondence, 1896–1899," frames 0754–73, reel 1, 81–82.

50. "Correspondence, 1896–1899," frames 0754–73, reel 1, 81–82.

51. See Hersey and Sutter, *My Work Is That of Conservation*.

52. Richard Pliant termed Carver the "Poor People's Scientist." He was a political scientist and professor at Washington University in St. Louis and also a descendant of the family who enslaved Carver and his parents. Pliant was responsible for the monument to Carver that was established in Missouri. See also Burchard, *George Washington Carver: For His Time and Ours*.

53. Carver, The Need for Scientific Ag in the South, 1–2.

54. Kremer, *George Washington Carver: In His Own Words*, 102.

55. Carver, "Hints to Southern Farmers," 351.

56. George Washington Carver, "How to Make and Save Money on the Farm," Bulletin No. 39, Experiment Station, Tuskegee Normal and Industrial Institute, 1927; Carver, "Twelve Ways to Meet the New Economic Conditions Here in the South," Bulletin No. 33, Experiment Station, Tuskegee Normal and Industrial Institute, 1917.

57. George Washington Carver, "How to Build Up Worn Out Soils," Bulletin No. 6, Experiment Station, Tuskegee Normal and Industrial Institute, 1905, Ibid., 4–6.

58. F. H. Cardoza, "The San Jose Scale in Alabama," Bulletin No. 9, Experiment Station, Tuskegee Normal and Industrial Institute, 1906, 1.

59. George Washington Carver, "How to Cook Cow Peas," Bulletin No. 13, Experiment Station, Tuskegee Normal and Industrial Institute, 1908.

60. The moveable school had many names, from the Jesup Wagon, to the Knapp Agricultural Truck, to the Booker T. Washington Agricultural School on Wheels.

61. Jones, "Role of Tuskegee Institute," 258.

62. Carver, "How to Build Up Worn Out Soils," 4.

63. Carver, "Need of Scientific Agriculture in the South," 3.

64. Carver, George W. The Need of Scientific Agriculture in the South, in *Farmers' Leaflet*, no. 7, April 1902, 1.

65. Holmgren, *Permaculture: Principles and Pathways Beyond Sustainability*, Hepburn, Victoria: Holmgren Design Services, 2002, xix.

66. Corn was even more damaging to the soil than cotton. See Hersey and Sutter, *My Work Is That of Conservation*, 60.

67. Douglas Blackmon, Slavery Under another Name: The Re-Enslavement of Black Americans from the Civil War to World War II. New York: Anchor Publishing.

68. Hersey and Sutter, *My Work Is That of Conservation*, 78.

69. Carver, "How to Build Up Worn Out Soils," 5.

70. George Washington Carver, "Some Cercosporae, of Macon County, Alabama," Bulletin No. 42, Experiment Station, Tuskegee Normal and Industrial Institute, 1901, 8.

71. George Washington Carver, "How to Build Up and Maintain the Virgin Fertility of Our Soils," Bulletin No. 42, Experiment Station, Tuskegee Normal and Industrial Institute, 1936, 5.

72. Carver, "How to Build Up Worn Out Soils," 3.

73. George Washington Carver, "Possibilities of the Sweet Potato in Macon County, Alabama," Bulletin No. 17, Experiment Station, Tuskegee Normal and Industrial Institute, 1910, 1.

74. George Washington Carver, "Some Possibilities of the Cow Pea in Macon County, Alabama," Bulletin No. 19, Experiment Station, Tuskegee Normal and Industrial Institute, 1910, 1.

75. George Washington Carver, "Three Delicious Meals Every Day for the Farmer," Bulletin No. 32, Experiment Station, Tuskegee Normal and Industrial Institute, 1916, 4–6.

76. For a complete list of Washington's inventions, see https://www.tuskegee.edu/support-tu/george-washington-carver/carver-peanut-products.

77. Hersey and Sutter, *My Work Is That of Conservation*, 171.

78. Hersey and Sutter, 62–63.

79. Du Bois, as quoted in Nembhard, *Collective Courage*, 162–63.

80. Joseph Jakubek and Spencer D. Wood, "Emancipatory Empiricism: The Rural Sociology of W.E.B DuBois," in *Sociology of Race and Ethnicity*, 2018, Vol. 4(1), 14–34.

81. No known copies of this study were salvaged. See Aptheker, *Contributions by W. E. B. Du Bois*; and Rabaka, *Against Epistemic Apartheid*.

82. Jakubek and Wood, "Emancipatory Empiricism," 16.

83. This section benefits from Nembhard's research on African American economic cooperatives and the work on Du Bois.

84. Nembhard, *Collective Courage*, 1.

85. Nembhard, 99.

86. Du Bois, *Economic Co-operation among Negro Americans*, 10.

87. Du Bois, 10.

88. Du Bois, 25.

89. Nembhard, *Collective Courage*, 99.

90. Du Bois, *Dusk of Dawn*, 100.

91. Du Bois, 100.

92. Du Bois, 108.

93. Du Bois, 106.

94. Du Bois, 106.

95. Du Bois, 106.

96. Du Bois, 106.

97. Du Bois, 108.

98. Du Bois, 106.

99. Du Bois, 107.

100. Du Bois, 107.

101. *The Crisis*, SIV September, 1917, 215.

102. See DeMarco, 135; Nembhard, *Collective Courage*, xxx; Lewis, *W. E. B. Du Bois: A Biography 1868-1963*; and Alexander, *W. E. B. Du Bois: An American Intellectual and Activist*.

103. Nembhard, *Collective Courage*, 103.

104. Du Bois, *Dusk of Dawn*, 759.

105. Nembhard, *Collective Courage*, 22. Two cooperatives that Du Bois referenced were the Consumers' Cooperative Trading Company in Gary, Ind., and the Ladies' Auxiliary to the Brotherhood of Sleeping Car Porters.

106. Du Bois, *Dusk of Dawn*, 105.

107. Du Bois, 107.

108. Du Bois, *The Crisis*, 1919, 50.

109. Du Bois, 1933, 1237.

110. *The Crisis*, December 1919, 48.

111. Nembhard, *Collective Courage*, 74.

112. See Friedland, "Commodity System Analysis."

CHAPTER 2

1. "Progress Report: Self-Help Campaign against Hunger," National Council of Negro Women Inc., June 1969 (Madison Measure for Measure Records, 1965–77: box 1, folder 15, Wisconsin Historical Society Archives, Madison), accessed September 11, 2014.

2. See Lee, *For Freedom's Sake*.

3. Seasonal schools offered six seasons of segregated education in December–March, while the planting and harvesting season usually started in early March, weather permitting.

4. See McMillen, *Dark Journey*.

5. See Bracey, *Fannie Lou Hamer*.

6. See Nelson, *Body and Soul*. See also Nelson, *Women of Color and the Reproductive Rights Movement*.

7. Jones and Eubanks, *Ain't Gonna Let Nobody Turn Me Around*, 259.

8. Cobb, *Most Southern Place on Earth*, 243.

9. Lee, *For Freedom's Sake*, 155. See also McGuire, *At the Dark End of the Street*, 192–95.

10. David Cunningham argues that the relationship between the KKK, or related and similarly violent racist organizations, and law enforcement ranged from direct support, to partnerships, to departments being infiltrated and Klansmen holding positions such as sheriff and police chief. See Cunningham, *Klansville, U.S.A.*

11. Fannie Lou Hamer, "Testimony before the Credentials Committee," Democratic National Convention, Atlantic City, N.J., August 22, 1964. Speech transcripts in Parker, *The Speeches of Fannie Lou Hamer: To Tell It Like it Is*, 42–45.

12. See Hamlet, "Fannie Lou Hamer."

13. There were other efforts to address health problems and malnutrition in Mississippi and in the South. See Jordan, "Fighting for the Child Development Group of Mississippi"; Green, "Saving Babies in Memphis"; and de Jong, Plantation Politics."

14. "Notes in the News: Going Hungry for Freedom," *Progressive* 32, June 6, 1968 (Madison Measure for Measure Records, 1965–77: box 1, folder 15, Wisconsin Historical Society Archives, Madison), accessed September 11, 2014.

15. U.S. Census Bureau, "General Population Characteristics," *Census of Population: 1960*, vol. 1, part 26, table 28 (Washington, D.C.: U.S. Department of Commerce, 1963), accessed September 11, 2014.

16. See Asch, *Senator and the Sharecropper.*

17. U.S. Census Bureau, "General Social and Economic Characteristics," *Census of Population: 1960*, vol. 1, part 26, table 88 (Washington, D.C.: U.S. Department of Commerce, 1963), accessed September 11, 2014.

18. Office of Economic Opportunity, "A Mississippi Summary," U.S. Senate Hearings before the Subcommittee on Employment, Manpower, and Poverty of the Committee on Labor and Public Welfare, 90th Congress, First Session, April 10, 1967: 1054.

19. Kotz, *Let Them Eat Promises*, 88.

20. See Gregory, "Second Great Migration." See also Wilkerson, *Warmth of Other Suns.*

21. See Boehm, *Making a Way out of No Way.*

22. U.S. Census Bureau, "General Social and Economic Characteristics."

23. Gramsci, *Selections from the Prison Notebooks*, 134.

24. Building on Gramsci's work on organic intellectuals, other scholars have used this framework. See Ransby, *Ella Baker and the Black Freedom Movement*; Lipsitz, *Life in the Struggle*; and D'Emilio, *Lost Prophet.*

25. "Notes in the News: Going Hungry for Freedom," *Progressive* 32, June 6, 1968.

26. "Notes in the News." For more information on the history of civil rights in Mississippi and on SNCC, see Dittmer, *Local People*; Charles Payne, *John Dittmer Local People: The Struggle for Civil Rights in Mississippi.* (Oakland, University of California Press, 2007); Crawford, Rouse, and Woods, *Women in the Civil Rights Movement*; Carson, *In Struggle*; Hogan, *Many Minds, One Heart*; and Holsaert et al., *Hands on the Freedom Plow.*

27. Megan Landauer and Jonathan Wolman, "Fannie Lou Hamer . . . Forcing a New Political Reality," *Daily Cardinal* (Madison, Wis.), October 8, 1971 (Madison Measure for Measure Records, 1965–77: box 1, folder 21, Wisconsin Historical Society Archives, Madison), accessed September 11, 2014.

28. Reynolds, *Black Farmers in America*, 4.

29. "Proposal for Community and Economic Development," January 13, 1969 (Madison Measure for Measure Records, 1965–77: box 1, folder 15, Wisconsin Historical Society Archives, Madison), accessed September 11, 2014.

30. "Fundraising Letter from Harry Belafonte for FFC," May 1969 (Fannie Lou Hamer Papers, 1966–78: box 1, folder 19, Amistad Research Center, Tulane University, New Orleans), accessed August 1, 2014.

31. Fallows, "Black Southern Farmers," 2.

32. The archives include instances of membership dues being one dollar per month per family and other instances of them being one dollar per year.

33. Franklynn Peterson, "Pig Banks Pay Dividends," *Commercial Appeal Mid-South Magazine* (Memphis, TN) January 7, 1973, 32 (Sweet Family Papers, 1970–77: box 7, folder 5, Wisconsin Historical Society Archives, Madison), accessed September 11, 2014.

34. "Madison Measure for Measure Brief on Freedom Farm Corporation and North Bolivar County Co-op Farm," n.d. (Madison Measure for Measure Records, 1965–77: box 1, folder 16, Wisconsin Historical Society Archives, Madison), accessed September 11, 2014.

35. Jean Carper, "A Report on Operation Daily Bread," National Council of Negro Women, October 1968 (Interreligious Foundation for Community Organization Records, 1966–84: box 48, folder 43, p. 11, Schomburg Center for Research in Black Culture, New York Public Library), accessed November 7, 2013.

36. Wendell Paris, personal communication, April 2013.

37. See Sherrod and Whitney, *Courage to Hope*.

38. Madison, "Mississippi's Secondary Boycott Statutes," 584.

39. Madison, 584.

40. "Progress Report: Self-Help Campaign against Hunger."

41. See Asch, *Senator and the Sharecropper*.

42. "Progress Report: Self-Help Campaign against Hunger."

43. Fannie Lou Hamer, "Freedom Farm Corporation, Annual Report," November 1972 (Madison Measure for Measure Records, 1965–77: box 1, folder 17, Wisconsin Historical Society Archives, Madison), accessed September 11, 2014.

44. FFC details from the "Progress Report: Self-Help Campaign against Hunger." Fannie Lou Hamer, "Freedom Farm Corporation: Status Report and Request for Funds," March 1973 (Fannie Lou Hamer Papers, 1966–78: box 10, Amistad Research Center, Tulane University, New Orleans), accessed August 1, 2014.

45. Fannie Lou Hamer, "Freedom Farm Corporation," June 1970 (Fannie Lou Hamer Papers, 1966–78: box 10, Amistad Research Center, Tulane University, New Orleans), accessed August 1, 2014.

46. Hamer, "Freedom Farm Corporation, Annual Report."

47. The accuracy of the number of pigs is contested in the primary documents.

48. "Sunflower County Freedom Farm Co-op," NCNW 1968, 8 (Fannie Lou Hamer Papers, 1966–78: box 10, Amistad Research Center, Tulane University, New Orleans), accessed August 1, 2014.

49. "Progress Report: Self-Help Campaign against Hunger."

50. See Nembhard, *Collective Courage*.

51. "Progress Report: Self-Help Campaign against Hunger."

52. Fannie Lou Hamer, "Fundraising Letter," May 15, 1970 (Fannie Lou Hamer Papers, 1966–78: box 1, Amistad Research Center, Tulane University, New Orleans), accessed August 1, 2014.

53. Peterson, "Pig Banks Pay Dividends."

54. Fannie Lou Hamer, "Freedom Farm Cooperatives, First Year Report," April 28, 1970 (Madison Measure for Measure Records, 1965–77: box 1, folder 17, Wisconsin Historical Society Archives, Madison), accessed September 11, 2014.

55. Fallows, "Black Southern Farmers," 2. As part of a national fundraising campaign to purchase land for housing, Lester Salamon, a teaching fellow in Harvard's Department of Government was listed as the FFC representative collecting funds on FFC's behalf. Journalist Fallows wrote an article in 1970 for the *Harvard Crimson* on the condition of housing in Sunflower County.

56. "Proposal for Community and Economic Development."

57. Fallows, "Black Southern Farmers."

58. Hamer, "Freedom Farm Cooperatives, First Year Report."

59. The FmHA is now known as the Rural Housing Service.

60. "Domestic Project: Mississippi Freedom Farm Cooperatives," n.d. (Madison Measure for Measure Records, 1965–77: box 1, folder 17, Wisconsin Historical Society Archives, Madison), accessed September 11, 2014.

61. Mills, *This Little Light of Mine*, 262.

62. Freedom Farm Corporation, "1972 Progress Report" (Fannie Lou Hamer Papers, 1966–78: box 10, Amistad Research Center, Tulane University, New Orleans), accessed August 1, 2014.

63. "1972 Progress Report."

64. See Jordan, "Fighting for the Child Development Group of Mississippi."

65. "Proposal for Community and Economic Development," January 13, 1969 (Madison Measure for Measure Records, 1965–77: box 1, folder 15, Wisconsin Historical Society Archives, Madison), accessed September 11, 2014. See also: Amy Jordan in . . . Annelise Orleck, Lisa Hazirjian (eds), The War on Poverty: A New Grassroots History, 1964-1980. (Athens: University of Georgia, 2011).

66. Joseph Harris, "Freedom Farm Corporation, Annual Report," January 23, 1973 (Madison Measure for Measure Records, 1965–77: box 1, folder 17, Wisconsin Historical Society Archives, Madison), accessed September 11, 2014.

67. "Proposal for Community and Economic Development"; January 13, 1969 (Madison Measure for Measure Records, 1965–77: box 1, folder 15, Wisconsin Historical Society Archives, Madison), accessed September 11, 2014. "Progress Report: Self-Help Campaign against Hunger."

68. "Madison Measure for Measure Brief on Freedom Farm Corporation and North Bolivar County Co-op Farm," n.d. (Madison Measure for Measure Records, 1965–77: box 1, folder 17, Wisconsin Historical Society Archives, Madison), accessed September 11, 2014.

69. "Northern Bolivar County Co-op Farm," n.d. (Eric Smith Papers, 1965–74: box 1, Wisconsin Historical Society Archives, Madison), accessed September 11, 2014.

70. Hamer, "Freedom Farm Corporation: Status Report and Request for Funds."

71. Jeff Goldstein, "Letter to S. L. Cobbs and Presbyterian Children's Home," July 18, 1968 (Madison Measure for Measure Records, 1965–77: box 1, folder 14, Wisconsin Historical Society Archives, Madison), accessed September 11, 2014. Based on the Food Stamp Act of 1964, the USDA had ceased to distribute surplus commodities in favor of providing food stamps, but the poor had to buy them. FFC established, managed, and administered the Sunflower County Food Stamp Fund under a committee of local citizens. Using funds raised from philanthropic organizations, it purchased and distributed the stamps and other donations. As the Measure for Measure report points out, by bringing federal money into Sunflower County, the program also benefited local merchants and storeowners.

72. Fannie Lou Hamer, "Letter to Madison Measure for Measure and Mrs. Eugene A. Wilkening," January 23, 1973 (Fannie Lou Hamer Papers, 1966–78: box 10, Amistad Research Center, Tulane University, New Orleans), accessed August 1, 2014.

73. National Council of Negro Women, Inc., "Self-Help Campaign Against Hunger, Progress Report," June 1969 (Madison Measure for Mea-

sure Records, 1965–77: box 1, folder 15, Wisconsin Historical Society Archives, Madison), accessed September 11, 2014, 7.

74. "Fundraising Letter from Harry Belafonte for FFC," May 1969 (Fannie Lou Hamer Papers, 1966–78: box 10, Amistad Research Center, Tulane University, New Orleans), accessed August 1, 2014.

75. "Sunflower County Freedom Farm Co-op," 1967 (Fannie Lou Hamer Papers, 1966–78: box 10, Amistad Research Center, Tulane University, New Orleans), accessed August 1, 2014.

76. "Progress Report: Self-Help Campaign against Hunger."

77. Jeff Goldstein, "Letter to Dorothy I. Height and National Council of Negro Women, Inc.," August 17, 1968 (Madison Measure for Measure Records, 1965–77: box 1, folder 14, Wisconsin Historical Society Archives, Madison), accessed September 11, 2014.

78. Joseph Harris, "Freedom Farm Corporation, Annual Report," January 23, 1973 (Madison Measure for Measure Records, 1965–77: box 1, folder 17, Wisconsin Historical Society Archives, Madison), accessed September 11, 2014.

79. Fannie Lou Hamer, "Freedom Farm Corporation: Status Report and Request for Funds," March 1973 (Fannie Lou Hamer Papers, 1966–78: box 10, Amistad Research Center, Tulane University, New Orleans), 3, accessed August 1, 2014.

80. Hamer, "Freedom Farm Corporation: Status Report and Request for Funds."

81. Minutes from Measure for Measure meeting, July 22, 1974 (Madison Measure for Measure Records, 1965–77: box 1, folder 17, p. 1, Wisconsin Historical Society Archives, Madison), accessed September 11, 2014.

CHAPTER 3

1. Bruce and Martha Fritz, "Report from Visit to NBCFC," January 1969 (Madison Measure for Measure, 1965–77: box 1, folder 18, Wisconsin Historical Society Archives, Madison), accessed October 2014.

2. Black, People and Plows Against Hunger, 1975, 6.

3. Washington, *Town Owned by Negroes*, 9125.

4. Quoted in Meier, "Booker T. Washington and the Town of Mound Bayou," 396.

5. Washington, *Town Owned by Negroes*, 9125.

6. Meier and Rudwick, *Along the Color Line*, 219.

7. Black, People and Plows, 19.

8. Meier, "Booker T. Washington and the Town of Mound Bayou," 398; Black, 18.

9. Black, 16.

10. See also: "Issues of Poverty, Exploitation, and Economic Justice" (no author) (Jan–July), accessed November 2014, http://www.crmvet.org/tim/tim65b.htm; Kelley, *Hammer and Hoe*; Honey, *Going Down Jericho Road*; Charles Payne, *John Dittmer Local People: The Struggle for Civil Rights in Mississippi* (Oakland, University of California Press, 2007); and Blackmon, *Slavery by Another Name*.

11. Cobb, The Most Southern Place on Earth, 269.

12. See Dittmer, *Local People*, and Payne, *I've Got the Light of Freedom*.

13. "The Tufts-Delta Health Center: A Progress Report," October 1968 (North Bolivar County Farm Cooperative Records, 1967–69: box 1, folder 4, Wisconsin Historical Society Archives, Madison), accessed October 2014.

14. H. Jack Geiger, "Tufts in Mississippi—The Delta Health Center, 1966" (North Bolivar County Farm Cooperative Records, 1967–69: box 1, folder 4, Wisconsin Historical Society Archives, Madison), accessed October 2014.

15. John Hatch, "Historical Sketch and Progress Report on the North Bolivar County Farm Cooperative," January 8, 1969 (North Bolivar County Farm Cooperative Records, 1967–69: box 1, folder 1, p. 1, Wisconsin Historical Society Archives, Madison), accessed October 2014.

16. Hatch, "Historical Sketch and Progress Report," 2.

17. Black, 7.

18. Hatch, "Historical Sketch and Progress Report," 2.

19. Hatch; "Historical Sketch and Progress Report"; "NBCFC Meeting Minutes," March 31, 1969 (North Bolivar County Farm Cooperative Records, 1967–69: box 1, folder 2, Wisconsin Historical Society Archives, Madison), accessed October 2014.

20. "NBCFC Meeting Minutes," March 31, 1969. (North Bolivar County Farm Cooperative Records, 1967–69: box 1, folder 2, Wisconsin Historical Society Archives, Madison), accessed October 2014.

21. "NBCFC Meeting Minutes," March 31, 1969 (North Bolivar County Farm Cooperative Records, 1967–69: box 1, folder 1, p. 3, Wisconsin Historical Society Archives, Madison), accessed October 2014.

22. "NBCFC Meeting Minutes," March 31, 1969, 2.

23. "NBCFC Meeting Minutes," March 31, 1969, 2.

24. Hatch, "Historical Sketch and Progress Report," 6.

25. Hatch, 7.

26. "NBCFC Meeting Minutes," March 31, 1969, 8.

27. "NBCFC Meeting Minutes," March 31, 1969, 9.

28. Madison Measure for Measure, "April 22, 1970 proposal to American Freedom from Hunger Foundation Inc." (Eric Smith Papers, 1965, 1974:

box 1, Wisconsin Historical Society Archives, Madison), accessed September 2014.

29. "NBCFC Meeting Minutes," October 25, 1968 (North Bolivar County Farm Cooperative Records, 1967–69: box 1, folder 2, Wisconsin Historical Society Archives, Madison), accessed October 2014.

CHAPTER 4

1. Wendell Paris, personal communication, 2014.

2. "Co-op Crackdown," editorial, *Nation*, November 22, 1980, 536.

3. See Piven and Cloward, *Poor People's Movements*, and de Jong, *You Can't Eat Freedom*.

4. See Joseph, *Black Power Movement*.

5. There are important histories that look at the roots in Cleveland (RAM), Detroit (the Boggses, RNA founders, third-party politics, etc.), New York, Oakland, and other cities, but Jeffries, *Bloody Lowndes*, focuses on Lowndes County, Alabama, black power as part of the SNCC civil rights struggles, and efforts toward political self-determination.

6. While traditions of black southern agricultural cooperatives existed (see Kelley, *Hammer and Hoe*), it is not clear from the archival material whether those involved with this new wave of cooperatives knew about or drew upon these precedents.

7. Quoted in McKnight, *Whistling in the Wind*, 26.

8. McKnight, 26.

9. "1978-1979 Twelfth Annual Report." Federation of Southern Cooperatives Papers: box 83, folder 14, p. 6 (Amistad Research Center, Tulane University, New Orleans), accessed September 27, 2013.

10. Federation of Southern Cooperatives/Land Assistance Fund, "Four Decades (1967–2007): Historical Review of the Federation of Southern Cooperatives/Land Assistance Fund," accessed March 17, 2014, http://www.federationsoutherncoop.com/fschistory/fsc4ohist.pdf.

11. *Cooperative Marketing Manual* (East Point, Ga.: Federation of Southern Cooperatives/Land Assistance Fund, 2006), 44.

12. Massey, "Federation of Southern Cooperatives," 38.

13. "1977-1978 Eleventh Annual Report, Suggested Issues of Discussion by State Caucuses and related material. Aug. 1978." Federation of Southern Cooperatives Papers: box 83, folder 13, p. 5 (Amistad Research Center, Tulane University, New Orleans), accessed September 27, 2013.

14. "1974–75 Eighth Annual Report," Federation of Southern Cooperatives Papers: box 83, folder 10, p. 1 (Amistad Research Center, Tulane University, New Orleans), accessed September 27, 2013.

15. Bethell, "In Defense of Freedom's Victory," 48. See also Slaughter, *New Battles over Dixie.*

16. These states are Alabama, Arkansas, Florida, Georgia, Kentucky, Louisiana, Mississippi, Missouri, North Carolina, South Carolina, Tennessee, Texas, and Virginia.

17. "Annual Report to the Board & Membership Meeting." Federation of Southern Cooperatives Papers: box 83, folder 6 (Amistad Research Center, Tulane University, New Orleans), accessed September 27, 2013.

18. See Bethell, "In Defense of Freedom's Victory"; Slaughter, *New Battles over Dixie*; and Wendell Paris, "Building Cooperatives in the Rural South," accessed September 2013, http://www.federationsoutherncoop.com /wendell.htm.

19. See Ashmore, *Carry It On.*

20. Ashmore, 202.

21. "1974-1975 Eight Annual Report." Federation of Southern Cooperatives Papers: box 83, folder 10 (Amistad Research Center, Tulane University, New Orleans), accessed September 27, 2013.

22. Massey, "Federation of Southern Cooperatives," 39.

23. Members who were not African American in Mississippi were indigenous/First Nations most in Kentucky, the Carolinas, and Tennessee were white; and most in Texas were Chicanos. Massey, "Federation of Southern Cooperatives," 39.

24. "1978-1979 Twelfth Annual Report." Federation of Southern Cooperatives Papers: box 83, folder 14, p. 25 (Amistad Research Center, Tulane University, New Orleans), accessed September 27, 2013.

25. "1974-1975 Eight Annual Report." Federation of Southern Cooperatives Papers: box 83, folder 10, p. 2 (Amistad Research Center, Tulane University, New Orleans), accessed September 27, 2013.

26. "1974-1975 Eight Annual Report." Federation of Southern Cooperatives Papers: box 83, folder 10, p. 2 (Amistad Research Center, Tulane University, New Orleans), accessed September 27, 2013.

27. "1978-1979 Twelfth Annual Report." Federation of Southern Cooperatives Papers: box 83, folder 14, p. 11 (Amistad Research Center, Tulane University, New Orleans), accessed September 27, 2013.

28. "1978-1979 Twelfth Annual Report." Federation of Southern Cooperatives Papers: box 83, folder 14, p. 11 (Amistad Research Center, Tulane University, New Orleans), accessed September 27, 2013.

29. "Board of Directors Meeting. November 17, 1973." Federation of Southern Cooperatives Papers: box 84, folder 47, p. 19 (Amistad Research Center, Tulane University, New Orleans), accessed September 27, 2013.

30. "1972 Annual Report." Federation of Southern Cooperatives Papers: box 83, folder 7, p. 4. Amistad Research Center, Tulane University, New Orleans), accessed September 27, 2013.

31. "1978-1979 Twelfth Annual Report." Federation of Southern Cooperatives Papers: box 83, folder 14, p. 17 (Amistad Research Center, Tulane University, New Orleans), accessed September 27, 2013.

32. "1974-1975 Eight Annual Report." Federation of Southern Cooperatives Papers: box 83, folder 10, p. 1 (Amistad Research Center, Tulane University, New Orleans), accessed September 27, 2013.

33. "1974-1975 Eighth Annual Report," Federation of Southern Cooperatives Papers: box 83, folder 10, p. 12 (Amistad Research Center, Tulane University, New Orleans), accessed September 27, 2013.

34. Paris, "Building Cooperatives in the Rural South." http://www.federationsoutherncoop.com/coopinfo/paris92.htm (accessed October, 2016).

35. "Executive Director's Report, 1969," Federation of Southern Cooperatives Papers: box 83, folder 3, p. 32 (Amistad Research Center, Tulane University, New Orleans), accessed September 27, 2013.

36. "1978-79. Twelfth Annual Report." Federation of Southern Cooperatives Papers: box 83, folder 14, p. 11 (Amistad Research Center, Tulane University, New Orleans), accessed September 27, 2013.

37. "1978-1979 Twelfth Annual Report." Federation of Southern Cooperatives Papers: box 83, folder 14, p. 25 (Amistad Research Center, Tulane University, New Orleans), accessed September 27, 2013.

38. Cooperative Marketing Strategies, 23, http://www.federationsoutherncoop.com/files%20home%20page/Marketing%20Manual%2011a.pdf, accessed February 2014.

39. Cooperative Marketing Strategies, 26.

40. "1974-1975 Annual Report," Federation of Southern Cooperatives Papers: box 83, folder 10, p. 12 (Amistad Research Center, Tulane University, New Orleans), accessed September 27, 2013.

41. "1976-1977 Annual Report, 1976-77," Federation of Southern Cooperatives Papers: box 83, folder 10, p. 2 (Amistad Research Center, Tulane University, New Orleans), accessed September 27, 2013.

42. "1971 Annual Report," Federation of Southern Cooperatives Papers: box 83, folder 6, p. 8 (Amistad Research Center, Tulane University, New Orleans), accessed September 27, 2013.

43. de Jong, *You Can't Eat Freedom*, 144-46.

44. "1978-1979 Annual Report," Federation of Southern Cooperatives Papers: box 83, folder 14, p. 11 (Amistad Research Center, Tulane University, New Orleans), accessed September 27, 2013.

45. "Annual Report," Federation of Southern Cooperatives Papers: box 84, folder 47, p. 19 (Amistad Research Center, Tulane University, New Orleans), accessed September 27, 2013.

46. "May 1, 1969-July 31, 1970-Summary of Operations for fifteen Month Period." Federation of Southern Cooperatives Papers: box 83, folder 4, p. 19 (Amistad Research Center, Tulane University, New Orleans), accessed September 27, 2013.

47. "1978-1979 Twelfth Annual Report," Federation of Southern Cooperatives Papers: box 83, folder 14, p. 17 (Amistad Research Center, Tulane University, New Orleans), accessed September 27, 2013.

48. "1974-1975 Eight Annual Report." Federation of Southern Cooperatives Papers: box 83, folder 10, p. 41 (Amistad Research Center, Tulane University, New Orleans), accessed September 27, 2013.

49. "1974-1975 Eight Annual Report." Federation of Southern Cooperatives Papers: box 83, folder 10, p. 39 (Amistad Research Center, Tulane University, New Orleans), accessed September 27, 2013.

50. "1978-1979 Twelfth Annual Report." Federation of Southern Cooperatives Papers: box 83, folder 14, p. 32 (Amistad Research Center, Tulane University, New Orleans), accessed September 27, 2013.

51. A New Life Stirs in Alabama Soil: Hundreds of poor farmers in the Heart of the Black Belt are Finding Hope in a forceful Co-op. *Black Enterprise*, October 1970, 40.

52. Same as above. No author listed. 40.

53. "Letter from Wilbert Guillory of Grand Marie Vegetable Producers Cooperative Inc. to Phil Littlejohn of IFCO," September 15, 1972 (Interreligious Foundation for Community Organization Records, 1966–84: box 28, folder 45 (Schomburg Center for Research in Black Culture, New York Public Library), accessed November 2014.

54. "1978-1979 Twelfth Annual Report." Federation of Southern Cooperatives Papers: box 83, folder 6, pp. 8–9 (Amistad Research Center, Tulane University, New Orleans), accessed October 2014.

55. "Co-op Crackdown," 536.

56. Vodicka, "Federation of Southern Cooperatives under Siege," 19.

57. Vodicka, 19.

58. Vodicka, 20.

59. Vodicka, 20.

60. Vodicka, 20.

61. As a community leader, Rev. Paris was both a member of the leadership of the Federation of Southern Cooperatives and active with the Sumpter County coalition. Whites took this as a sign that FSC was overtly political, an

idea that was unsubstantiated. Paris was active in a number of specific roles.

62. Quoted in Vodicka, 21.

63. "1971, Annual Report to the Board and Membership of F.S.C." Federation of Southern Cooperatives Papers: box 83, folder 6, pp. 8–9 (Amistad Research Center, Tulane University, New Orleans), accessed October 2014.

64. Gaillard, *Cradle of Freedom*, 311.

65. Gaillard, 311.

66. See Rosengarten, Our Promised Land in Southern Exposure, vol. 2, no. 9.

67. Ashmore, *Carry it On*, 218. See also: Miles, *Black Cooperatives*, 1968, and Rushton, Rosengarten, *Our Promised Land*, 43, and Ward and Geiger, *Out in the Rural.*

68. See Daniel, *Dispossession*, for an account of the origins of USDA Cooperative Extension program.

69. "Charles O. Prejean, 1971 Annual Report to the Board and Membership of F.S.C." Federation of Southern Cooperatives Papers: box 83, folder 6, pp. 7–8 (Amistad Research Center, Tulane University, New Orleans), accessed October 2014.

CHAPTER 5

1. See Thompson, *Whose Detroit?*. See also Georgakas and Surkin, *Detroit, I Do Mind Dying*; Bates, *Making of Black Detroit*; Smith, *Dancing in the Street*; Sugrue, *Origins of the Urban Crisis*; and Geschwender, *Class, Race, and Worker Insurgency.*

2. See Sugrue, *Origins of the Urban Crisis.*

3. U.S. Census Bureau, "1960 to 1990 Census Count by for Michigan and Subcounties," https://www.michigan.gov/documents/MCD1960-1990C_33608_7.pdf, accessed August 2015.

4. http://www.census.gov/quickfacts/table/PST045215/2622000.

5. Sheena Hairston, "A City without Chain Grocery Stores: National Retailers Are Steering Clear of Detroit, Leaving Independent Grocers to Serve the City's Hard-Hit Residents," CNN Money, July 22, 2009, http://money.cnn.com/2009/07/22/smallbusiness/detroit_grocery_stores.smb/index.htm.

6. Malik Yakini, personal communication, October 2009.

7. Yakini, October 2009.

8. Malik Yakini, personal communication, November 2016.

9. Malik Yakini, personal communication, November 2016.

10. Yakini, November 2016.

11. "Detroit Black Community Food Security Network's Recommendations on the Establishment, Structure, and Functioning of the Detroit Food Policy Council Recommendations," 1, http://detroitfoodpolicycouncil.net/sites/default/files/pdfs/DBCFSN_DETROIT_FOOD_POLICY_COUNCIL_RECOMMENDATIONS.pdf, accessed October 2013.

12. "About Us," Keep Growing Detroit, http://detroitagriculture.net/about, accessed October 2013.

13. Aba Ifeoma, personal communication, October 2009.

14. Linda, personal communication, October 2009.

15. Marilyn Nefer Ra Barber, personal communication, October 2009.

16. Kwamenah Mensah, personal communication, January 2009.

17. Mensah, January 2009.

18. Harrison, "City without Chain Grocery Stores."

19. Yakini, October 2009. The grocery stores that were around during his lifetime were Chatham, Farmer Jack's, Kroger, A&P, and Wrigley.

20. Ifeoma, October 2009.

21. Ebony Roberts, personal communication, October 2009.

22. Roberts, October 2009.

23. Yakini, October 2009.

24. Ifeoma, October 2009.

25. Yakini, October 2009.

26. Roberts, October 2009.

27. Tee Rushdan, personal communication, October 2009.

28. "Notes in the News: Going Hungry for Freedom," *Progressive* 32 (June 6, 1968).

29. Many, if not most, cities now have organizations that address food access and food security for underserved communities of color. Two examples are Rid-All in Cleveland and the BLK Projek in the Bronx (New York City).

30. Ifeoma, October 2009.

31. Mensah, October 2009.

32. Ifeoma, October 2009.

33. Yakini, October, 2009.

34. See Linda C. Tapsell, Elizabeth P. Neale, Ambika Satija, Frank B. Hu, "Food, Nutrients, and Dietary Patterns: Interconnections and Implication for Dietary Guidelines." *Advance in Nutrition* 7, no. 3 (May 1, 2016).

35. Russell Rothman, MD, MPP, Ryan Housam, BS, Hilary Weiss, BS, Dianne Davis, RD CDE, Rebecca Gregory, MS, RD CDE, Tebeb Gebretsadik, MPH, Ayumi Shintani, PhD, MPH, Tom A. Elasy, MD, MPH, "Patient Understanding of Food Labels: The Role of Literacy and Numeracy," *American Journal of Preventive Medicine* 31, no. 5 (November 2006): 391–98.

36. Roberts, October 2009.
37. Marilyn Nefer Ra Barber, October 2009.
38. Mensah, October 2009.
39. See LeDuff, *Detroit.*

CONCLUSION

1. Wood, *Roots of Black Power.* See also: Reid and Bennett, *Beyond Forty Acres and a Mule.*

Bibliography

PRIMARY SOURCES

Archival
Alabama
    Birmingham
        Birmingham Public Library
            Birmingham News, January 28, 1970
            Birmingham Post Herald, June 1968
            Civil Rights Digest, Summer 1968
            Montgomery Advertiser, January 10, 1911; January 14, 1911;
                December 1, 1911; January, 10, 1912; January 14, 1912;
                January 17, 1912
            Selma Times Journal, October 20, 1968
    Montgomery
        Alabama Department of State Archives
    Tuskegee
        Tuskegee University
            George Washington Carver Bulletins. Box 1
            Tuskegee Student, 1897
Louisiana
    New Orleans
        Tulane University
            Amistad Research Center
                Federation of Southern Cooperatives, 1967–83. Boxes 83–85
                    and 87.
                Fannie Lou Hamer Papers, 1966–78. Boxes 1 and 10.
Mississippi
    Jackson
        Fannie Lou Townsend Hamer Papers. Tougaloo College Civil Rights
            Collection. T/012/Boxes 1–3.
        Mississippi Department of Archives and History
New York
    Schomburg Center for Research in Black Culture, New York Public
        Library, New York, N.Y.
        Interreligious Foundation for Community Organization
            Records, 1966–84. ScMg227. Boxes 28, 46, and 48.

Wisconsin
 Madison
  Wisconsin Historical Archives
   Lee Bankhead Papers, 1962–71. Box 1.
   Hamer, Fannie Lou. University of Wisconsin–Madison. 1976.
    Keynote Address. Tape 782A, nos. 1 and 2. Madison
    Measure for Measure Records, 1965–77.
   Madison Measure for Measure Records, 1965–77. Box 1.
   North Bolivar County Farm Cooperative records, 1967–69. Box 1.
   George Washington Carver Papers at Tuskegee Institute,
    microfilm, series 2: "Correspondence, 1896–99," frames
    0754–73, reel 1, 81–82, Wisconsin Historical Society
    Archives, Madison, accessed October 2015.
   Poor People's Corporation Records, 1960–67. Box 2, folder 22.
   Eric Smith Papers, 1965–74. Box 1.
   Sweet Family Papers, 1970–77. Box 7.

SECONDARY SOURCES

Abron, JoNina M. "'Serving the People': The Survival Programs of the
 Black Panther Party." In *The Black Panther Party [Reconsidered]*,
 edited by Charles E. Jones, 177–92. Baltimore: Black Classic Press, 1998.
Alexander, Shawn Leigh. *W. E. B. Du Bois: An American Intellectual and
 Activist*. Lanham, Md.: Rowman & Littlefield, 2015.
Ali, Omar H. *In the Lion's Mouth: Black Populism in the New South,
 1886–1900*. Jackson: University Press of Mississippi, 2010.
Alkebulan, Paul. *Survival Pending Revolution: History of the Black Panther
 Party*. Tuscaloosa: University of Alabama Press, 2007.
Anderson, Devery S. *Emmett Till: The Murder That Shocked the World and
 Propelled the Civil Rights Movement*. Jackson: University of Mississippi
 Press, 2015.
Aptheker, Herbert, ed. *Contributions by W. E. B. Du Bois in Government
 Publications and Proceedings [1–3]*. Millwood, N.Y.: Kraus-Thomson, 1980.
Asch, Chris Meyers. *The Senator and the Sharecropper: The Freedom Struggles
 of James O. Eastland and Fannie Lou Hamer*. New York: New Press, 2008.
Ashmore, Susan. *Carry It On: The War on Poverty and the Civil Rights
 Movement in Alabama, 1964–1972*. Athens: University of Georgia Press,
 2008.
Balvanz, Peter, Morgan L. Barlow, Lillianne M. Lewis, Kari Samuel,
 William Owens, Donna L. Parker, Molly De Marco, Robin Crowder,
 Yarbrough Williams, Dorathy Barker, Alexandra Lightfoot, Alice

Ammerman. "'The Next Generation, That's Why We Continue to Do What We Do': African American Farmers Speak about Experiences with Land Ownership and Loss in North Carolina." *Journal of Agriculture, Food Systems, and Community Development* 1, no. 3 (2011): 67–88.

Baptist, Edward E. *The Half Has Never Been Told: Slavery and the Making of American Capitalism.* New York: Basic Books, 2014.

Barickman, B. J. "'A Bit of Land, Which They Call Roça': Slave Provision Grounds in the Bahian Recôncavo, 1780–1860." *The Hispanic American Historical Review* 74, no. 4 (November 1994): 649–87.

Bates, Beth Tompkins. *The Making of Black Detroit in the Age of Henry Ford.* Chapel Hill: University of North Carolina Press, 2014.

Beeby, James M. *Populism in the South Revisited: New Interpretations and New Departures.* Jackson: University Press of Mississippi, 2012.

Bethell, Thomas. "In Defense of Freedom's Victory! The Ordeal of the Federation of Southern Cooperatives," *Southern Exposure: Stories of Triumph and Survival,* September/October 1982, 48–59.

Black, Herbert. "People and Plows Against Hunger: Self-help Experiment in a Rural Community," Boston: Marlborough House, 1975.

Blackmon, Douglas. *Slavery by Another Name: The Re-Enslavement of Black Americans from the Civil War to World War II.* New York: Anchor Books, 2008.

Boehm, Lisa Krissoff. *Making a Way Out of No Way: African American Women and the Second Great Migration.* Jackson: University Press of Mississippi, 2009.

Bracey, Earnest N. *Fannie Lou Hamer: The Life of a Civil Rights Icon.* Jefferson, N.C.: McFarland, 2011.

Branch, Taylor. *Parting the Waters: America in the King Years 1954–63.* New York: Simon & Schuster, 1989.

Brooks, Maegan Parker, and Davis W. Houck, eds. *The Speeches of Fannie Lou Hamer: To Tell It Like It Is.* Jackson: University Press of Mississippi, 2011.

Brotz, Howard, ed. *African-American Social and Political Thought: 1850–1920.* New Brunswick, N.J.: Transaction Publishers, 2009.

Burchard, Peter Duncan. *George Washington Carver: For His Time and Ours.* Special History Study: Natural History Related to George Washington Carver National Monument. Diamond, Mo.: National Parks Service, United States Department of the Interior, 2005.

Campbell, Thomas Monroe. *The Movable School Goes to the Negro Farmer.* New York: Arno Press and the New York Times, 1969.

Carney, Judith A. *Black Rice: The African Origins of Rice Cultivation in the Americas.* Cambridge, Mass.: Harvard University Press, 2002.

———. "'With Grains in Her Hair': Rice in Colonial Brazil." *Slavery and Abolition* 25, no. 1 (2004): 1–27.

Carney, Judith A., and Richard Nicholas Rosomoff. *In the Shadow of Slavery: Africa's Botanical Legacy in the Atlantic World*. Berkeley: University of California Press, 2009.

Carson, Clayborne. *In Struggle: SNCC and the Black Awakening of the 1960s*. Cambridge, Mass.: Harvard University Press, 1995.

Carver, George Washington. "A Few Hints to Southern Farmers." *Southern Workman and Hampton School Record* 75, no. 1 (1899): 351.

———. "The Need of Scientific Agriculture in the South." *Monthly Review of Reviews* 25 (1902): 321.

Cha-Jua, Sundiata Keita. *America's First Black Town: Brooklyn, Illinois, 1830–1915*. Urbana: University of Illinois Press, 2002.

Cobb, James C. *The Most Southern Place on Earth: The Mississippi Delta and the Roots of Regional Identity*. New York: Oxford University Press, 1992.

Cooper, Davina. "Intersectional Travel through Everyday Utopias." In *Intersectionality and Beyond: Law, Power, and the Politics of Location*, edited by Emily Grabham, Davina Cooper, Jane Krishnadas, and Didi Herman, 299–325. New York: Routledge-Cavendish, 2009.

Crawford, Vicki L., Jacqueline Anne Rouse, and Barbara Woods, eds. *Women in the Civil Rights Movement: Trailblazers and Torchbearers, 1941–1965*. Bloomington: University of Indiana Press, 1993.

Cronon, E. David. *Black Moses: The Story of Marcus Garvey and the Universal Negro Improvement Association*. Madison: University of Wisconsin Press, 1969.

Cunningham, David. *Klansville, U.S.A.: The Rise and Fall of the Civil Rights-Era Ku Klux Klan*. New York: Oxford University Press, 2013.

Daniel, Pete. *Breaking the Land: The Transformation of Cotton, Tobacco, and Rice Cultures since 1880*. Urbana: University of Illinois Press, 1985.

———. *Dispossession: Discrimination against African American Farmers in the Age of Civil Rights*. Chapel Hill: University of North Carolina Press, 2013.

Dann, Martin. "Black Populism: A Study of the Colored Farmers' Alliance through 1891." *Journal of Ethnic Studies* 2, no. 3 (1974): 58–71.

de Jong, Greta. *A Different Day: African American Struggles for Justice in Rural Louisiana, 1900–1970*. Chapel Hill: University of North Carolina, 2002.

———. "Plantation Politics: The Tufts-Delta Health Center and Intraracial Class Conflict in Mississippi, 1965–1972." In *The War on Poverty: A New Grassroots History, 1964–1980*, edited by Annelise Orleck and Lisa Hazirjian, 256–79. Athens: University of Georgia Press, 2011.

———. "'With the Aid of God and the F.S.A.': The Louisiana Farmers' Union and the African American Freedom Struggle in the New Deal Era." *Journal of Social History* 34, no. 1 (2000): 105–39.

———. *You Can't Eat Freedom: Southerners and Social Justice after the Civil Rights Movement.* Chapel Hill: University of North Carolina Press, 2016.

D'Emilio, John. *Lost Prophet: The Life and Times of Bayard Rustin.* Chicago: University of Chicago Press, 2004.

Demissie, Ejigou. "A History of Black Farm Operators in Maryland." *Agriculture and Human Values* 9, no. 1 (1992): 22–30.

Denby, Charles. *Indignant Heart: A Black Worker's Journal.* Detroit: Wayne State University Press, 1989.

Dittmer, John. *Local People: The Struggle for Civil Rights in Mississippi.* Urbana: University of Illinois Press, 1994.

Du Bois, W. E. B. *Dusk of Dawn: An Essay toward an Autobiography of a Race Concept.* New York: Oxford University Press, 1940.

———, ed. *Economic Co-operation among Negro Americans.* Report of a Study made by Atlanta University, under the Patronage of the Carnegie Institution of Washington, D.C., together with the Proceedings of the 12th Conference for the Study of the Negro Problems, held at Atlanta University, on Tuesday, May the 28th, 1907. Atlanta: Atlanta University Press, 1907.

———, *The Crisis*, SIV September, 1917, p. 215.

Dyson, Michael Eric. *I May Not Get There with You: The True Martin Luther King Jr.* New York: Free Press, 2001.

Escobar, Arturo, and Wendy Harcourt. "Practices of Difference: Introducing Women and the Politics of Place." In *Women and the Politics of Place*, 1–19. Bloomfield, Conn.: Kumarian, 2005.

Evans, Sara M., and Harry C. Boyte. *Free Spaces: The Sources of Democratic Change in America.* New York: Harper & Row, 1986.

Fallows, James M. "Black Southern Farmers Need Money to Buy Land in Mississippi for Co-op." *Harvard Crimson* (March 10, 1970), https://www.thecrimson.com/article/1970/3/10/black-southern-farmers-need-money-to/.

"The Farming Problem in the Black Belt," *Southern Workman* 30 (April 1901): 189–191.

Federer, William J. *George Washington Carver: His Life and Faith in His Own Words.* St. Louis: Amerisearch, 2002.

Ferguson, Karen J. "Caught in 'No Man's Land': The Negro Cooperative Demonstration Service and the Ideology of Booker T. Washington, 1900–1918." *Agricultural History Society* 72, no. 1 (Winter 1998): 33–54.

Fields-Black, Edda L. *Deep Roots: Rice Farmers in West Africa and the African Diaspora.* Bloomington: Indiana University Press, 2014.

Finlay, Mark R. "Old Efforts at New Uses: A Brief History of Chemurgy and the American Search for Biobased Materials." *Journal of Industrial Ecology* 7, nos. 3–4 (2004): 33–46.

Friedland, William H. "Commodity System Analysis: An Approach to the Sociology of Agriculture." In *Research in Rural Sociology and Development*, edited by Harry K. Schwarzweller, 221–236. London: JAI Press, 1984.

Futrell, Robert, and Pete Simi. "Free Spaces, Collective Identity, and the Persistence of U.S. White Power Activism." *Social Problems* 51 (2004): 16–42.

Gaillard, Frye. *Cradle of Freedom: Alabama and the Movement That Changed America*. Tuscaloosa: University of Alabama Press, 2004.

Garrow, David. *Bearing the Cross: Martin Luther King Jr. and the Southern Christian Leadership Conference*. New York: Random House, 1988.

Georgakas, Dan, and Marvin Surkin. *Detroit, I Do Mind Dying: A Study in Urban Revolution*. Brooklyn, N.Y.: South End Press, 1999.

Geschwender, James. *Class, Race, and Worker Insurgency: The League of Revolutionary Black Workers*. Cambridge: Cambridge University Press, 1977.

Gilbert, Carlene, and Quinn Eli. *Homecoming: The Story of African American Farmers*. Boston: Beacon Press, 2000.

Gilbert, Jess, Gwen Sharp, and M. Sindy Felin. "The Loss and Persistence of Black-Owned Farms and Farmland: A Review of the Research Literature and Its Implications." *Southern Rural Sociology* 18, no. 2 (2002): 1–30.

Glaser, Barney G., and Judith Holton. "Remodeling Grounded Theory." *Forum: Qualitative Social Research* 5, no. 2 (2004). http://www .qualitative-research.net/index.php/fqs/article/view/607/1316.

Gramsci, Antonio. *Selections from the Prison Notebooks of Antonio Gramsci*. Edited and translated by Quintin Hoare and Geoffrey Nowell-Smith. London: Lawrence & Wishart, 1971.

Gray, Karen A. "Community Land Trusts in the United States." *Journal of Community Practice* 16, no. 1 (2008): 65–78.

Gray, Lewis Cecil. *History of Agriculture in the Southern United States to 1860*. 2 vols. Washington, D.C.: Carnegie Institution of Washington, 1933.

Green, Laurie. "Saving Babies in Memphis: The Politics of Race, Health, and Hunger during the War on Poverty." In *The War on Poverty: A New Grassroots History, 1964–1980*, edited by Annelise Orleck and Lisa Hazirjian, 133–158. Athens: University of Georgia Press, 2011.

Gregory, James N. "The Second Great Migration: A Historical Overview." In *African American Urban History since World War II*, edited by Joe Trotter and Ken Kusmer, 19–28. Chicago: University of Chicago Press, 2009.

Groch, Sharon. "Free Spaces: Creating Oppositional Consciousness in the Disability Rights Movement." In *Oppositional Consciousness: The Subjective Roots of Social Protest,* edited by Jane J. Mansbridge and Aldon Morris, 65–98. Chicago: University of Chicago Press, 2001.

Hahn, Steven. *A Nation under Our Feet: Black Political Struggles in the Rural South from Slavery to the Great Migration.* Cambridge, Mass.: Belknap Press of Harvard University Press, 2003.

Haley, Sarah. *No Mercy Here: Gender, Punishment, and the Making of Jim Crow Modernity.* Chapel Hill: University of North Carolina Press, 2016.

Hamlet, Janice D. "Fannie Lou Hamer: The Unquenchable Spirit of the Civil Rights Movement." *Journal of Black Studies* 26, no. 5 (1996): 560–76.

Harlan, Louis R. *Booker T. Washington.* Vol. 1, *The Making of a Black Leader, 1856–1901.* New York: Oxford University Press, 1975.

———. *Booker T. Washington.* Vol. 2, *The Wizard of Tuskegee, 1901–1915.* New York: Oxford University Press, 1986.

Harrison, Alferdteen. *Piney Woods School: An Oral History.* Jackson: University of Mississippi Press, 1983.

Height, Dorothy. *Open Wide the Freedom Gates: A Memoir.* New York: Public Affairs, 2005.

Hersey, Mark, and Paul Sutter. *My Work Is That of Conservation: An Environmental Biography of George Washington Carver.* Athens: University of Georgia Press, 2011.

Hill, Robert A., ed. *The Marcus Garvey and Universal Negro Improvement Association Papers.* Vol. 7, *The Caribbean Diaspora, 1910–1920.* Durham, N.C.: Duke University Press, 2011.

———. *The Marcus Garvey and Universal Negro Improvement Association Papers.* Vol. 11, *The Caribbean Diaspora, 1910–1920.* Durham, N.C.: Duke University Press, 2011.

Hogan, Wesley. *Many Minds, One Heart: SNCC's Dream for a New America.* Chapel Hill: University of North Carolina Press, 2009.

Holsaert, Faith S., Martha Prescod Norman Noonan, Judy Richardson, Betty Garman Robinson, Jean Smith Young, and Dorothy M. Zellner, eds. *Hands on the Freedom Plow: Personal Accounts of Women in SNCC.* Urbana: University of Illinois Press, 2012.

Honey, Michael K. *Going Down Jericho Road: The Memphis Strike, Martin Luther King's Last Campaign.* New York: W.W. Norton & Company, 2011.

Honey, Michael K., and Pete Seeger. *Sharecroppers' Troubadour: John L. Handcox, the Southern Tenant Farmers' Union, and the African American Song Tradition.* New York: Palgrave Macmillan, 2013.

hooks, bell. *Sisters of the Yam: Black Women and Self-Recovery.* New York: Routledge, 2014.

Hunter, Tera, W. *To 'Joy My freedom: Southern Black Women's Lives and Labors after the Civil War.* Cambridge: Harvard University Press, 1998.

Hurt, R. Douglas, ed. *African American Life in the Rural South, 1900-1950.* Columbia: University of Missouri Press, 2011.

Kelley, *Hammer and Hoe*: Alabama Communists during the Great Depression: University of North Carolina Press; 2nd edition, 2015.

Jackson, Thomas. *From Civil Rights to Human Rights and the Struggle for Economic Justice.* Philadelphia: University of Pennsylvania Press, 2009.

Jakubek, Joseph, and Spencer D. Wood. "Emancipatory Empiricism: The Rural Sociology of W. E. B. Du Bois." *Sociology of Race and Ethnicity,* April 29, 2017.

Jeffries, Hasan Kwame. *Bloody Lowndes: Civil Rights and Black Power in Alabama's Black Belt.* New York: NYU Press, 2010.

Johnson, Charles S. *Shadow of the Plantation.* Chicago: University of Chicago Press, 1934.

Jones, Alethia, and Virginia Eubanks, eds. *Ain't Gonna Let Nobody Turn Me Around: Forty Years of Movement Building with Barbara Smith.* Albany, N.Y.: SUNY Press, 2014.

Jones, Allen W. "The Role of Tuskegee Institute in the Education of Black Farmers." *Journal of Negro History* 60, no. 3 (1975): 252-67.

Jones, William P. *The March on Washington: Jobs, Freedom, and the Forgotten History of Civil Rights.* New York: W.W. Norton & Company, 2014.

Jordan, Amy. "Fighting for the Child Development Group of Mississippi: Poor People." In *The War on Poverty: A New Grassroots History, 1964–1980,* edited by Annelise Orleck and Lisa Hazirjian, 208-307. Athens: University of Georgia, 2011.

Joseph, Peniel. *The Black Power Movement: Rethinking the Civil Rights-Black Power Era.* London: Routledge Press, 2006.

Joyner, Charles. *Down by the Riverside: A South Carolina Slave Community.* Urbana: University of Illinois Press, 1984.

Kelley, Robin D. G. *Hammer and Hoe: Alabama Communists during the Great Depression.* Chapel Hill: University of North Carolina, 2015.

Kirkby, Ryan J. "'The Revolution Will Not Be Televised': Community Activism and the Black Panther Party, 1966-1971." *Canadian Review of American Studies* 41, no. 1 (2011): 25-62.

Kotz, Nick. *Let Them Eat Promises: The Politics of Hunger in America.* Garden City, N.Y.: Anchor Books, 1971.

Kraft, Barbra R., Louis R. Harlan, and Raymond Smock, eds. *Booker T. Washington Papers.* Vol. 5, *1899-1900.* Urbana: University of Illinois Press, 1977.

Kremer, Gary R. *George Washington Carver: A Biography*. Santa Barbara, Calif.: Greenwood, 2011.

———. *George Washington Carver: In His Own Words*. Columbia: University of Missouri Press, 1987.

Lamont, Hammond, ed. *Negro Self-Help*. Tuskegee, Ala.: Tuskegee Institute Press, 1904.

LeDuff, Charlie. *Detroit: An American Autopsy*. Westminster, England: Penguin Books, 2014.

Lee, Chana Kai. *For Freedom's Sake: The Life of Fannie Lou Hamer*. Urbana: University of Illinois Press, 2000.

LeFlouria, Talitha L. *Chained in Silence: Black Women and Convict Labor in the New* South. Chapel Hill: University of North Carolina Press, 2015.

Lemann, Nicholas. *The Promised Land: The Great Black Migration and How It Changed America*. New York: Vintage Books, 1992.

Lewis, David Levering. *W. E. B. Du Bois: A Biography 1868–1963*. New York: Holt Paperbacks, 2009.

Lipsitz, George. *A Life in the Struggle: Ivory Perry and the Culture of Opposition*. Philadelphia: Temple University Press, 1995.

Lockley, Timothy J., ed. *Maroon Communities in South Carolina*. Columbia: University of South Carolina Press, 2009.

Lynn-Sherow, Bonnie. *Red Earth: Race and Agriculture in Oklahoma Territory*. Lawrence: University of Kansas Press, 2004.

Madison, Isaiah. "Mississippi's Secondary Boycott Statutes: Unconstitutional Deprivations of the Right to Engage in Peaceful Picketing and Boycotting." *Howard Law Journal* 18, no. 3 (1975): 584.

Mandle, Jay R. *The Roots of Black Poverty: The Southern Plantation Economy after the Civil War*. Durham, N.C.: Duke University Press, 1978.

Mantler, Gordon. *Power to the Poor: Black-Brown Coalition and the Fight for Economic Justice, 1960–1974*. Chapel Hill: University of North Carolina Press, 2015.

Marable, Manning, and Leigh Mullings. *Let Nobody Turn Us Around: Voices of Resistance, Reform, and Renewal*. Lanham, Md.: Rowman & Littlefield, 2003.

Marshall, F. Ray, and Lamond Godwin. *Cooperatives and Rural Poverty in the South*. Baltimore: Johns Hopkins Press, 1971.

Massey, David Dyar. "The Federation of Southern Cooperatives: Hard Times and High Hopes." *Southern Exposure* 2 (Autumn 1974): 38.

Masten, Ann S. "Resilience in Developing Systems: Progress and Promise as the Fourth Wave Rises." *Development and Psychopathology* 19 (2007): 921–30.

Mayberry, B. D. *The Role of Tuskegee University in the Origin, Growth, and Development of the Negro Cooperative Extension System, 1881–1990.* Tuskegee, Ala.: Tuskegee University Cooperative Extension Program, 1989.

McCutcheon, Priscilla. "Community Food Security 'For Us, by Us': The Nation of Islam and the Pan African Orthodox Christian Church." In *Cultivating Food Justice: Race, Class, and Sustainability,* edited by Alison Hope Alkon and Julian Agyeman, 177–96. Cambridge, Mass.: MIT Press, 2011.

———. "'Returning Home to Our Rightful Place': The Nation of Islam and Muhammed Farms." *Geoforum* 49 (2013): 61–70.

McGee, Leo, and Robert Boone. *The Black Rural Landowner—Endangered Species: Social, Political, and Economic Implications.* Westport, Conn.: Greenwood Press, 1979.

McGuire, Danielle. *At the Dark End of the Street: Black Women, Rape, and Resistance—a New History of the Civil Rights Movement from Rosa Parks to the Rise of Black Power.* New York: Alfred A. Knopf, 2010.

McKnight, A. J. *Whistling in the wind: The Autobiography of the Rev. A.J. McKnight, C.S. Sp.* Lafayette, LA: Southern Development Foundation, 1994.

McMillen, Neil R. *Dark Journey: Black Mississippians in the Age of Jim Crow.* Urbana: University of Illinois Press, 1990.

Meier, August. "Booker T. Washington and the Town of Mound Bayou." *Phylon* 15, no. 4 (1954): 339–40.

Miles, Michael. "Black Cooperatives." *The New Republic,* September, 1968, 21.

Millar, Floyd J. "Black Protest and White Leadership: A Note on the 'Colored Farmers' Alliance." *Phylon* 33, no. 2 (1972): 169–74.

Mills, Kay. *This Little Light of Mine: The Life of Fannie Lou Hamer (Civil Rights and Struggle).* Lexington: University Press of Kentucky, 2007.

Mintz, Sidney. *Tasting Food, Tasting Freedom: Excursions into Eating, Power, and the Past.* Boston: Beacon Press, 1997.

Moore, Jacqueline M. *Booker T. Washington, W. E. B. Du Bois, and the Struggle for Racial Uplift.* Lanham, Md.: SR Books, 2003.

Morris, Aldon. *The Scholar Denied: W. E. B. Du Bois and the Birth of Modern Sociology.* Berkeley: University of California Press, 2015.

Nelson, Alondra. *Body and Soul: The Black Panther Party and the Fight against Medical Discrimination.* Minneapolis: University of Minnesota Press, 2013.

Nelson, Jennifer. *Women of Color and the Reproductive Rights Movement.* New York: New York University Press, 2004.

Nembhard, Jessica. *Collective Courage: A History of African American Cooperative Economic Thought and Practice.* University Park: Pennsylvania State University Press, 2014.

Nixon, Rob. *Slow Violence and the Environmentalism of the Poor.* Cambridge, Mass.: Harvard University Press, 2013.

Norrell, Robert J. *Up from History: The Life of Booker T. Washington.* Cambridge, Mass.: Belknap Press of Harvard University Press, 2011.

Orleck, Annelise, and Lisa Gayle Hazirjian, eds. *The War on Poverty: A New Grassroots History 1964–1980.* Athens, Georgia: University of Georgia Press, 2011.

Painter, Nell Irvin. *Exodusters: Black Migration to Kansas after Reconstruction.* New York: Alfred A. Knopf, 1977.

Patel, Raj. "Survival Pending Revolution: What the Black Panthers Can Teach the US Food Movement." In *Food Movements Unite! Strategies to Transform Our Food Systems,* edited by Eric Holt-Gimenez, 115–37. Oakland, Calif.: Food First Books, 2011.

Payne, Charles. *I've Got the Light of Freedom: The Organizing Tradition and the Mississippi Freedom Struggle.* Berkeley: University of California Press, 1995.

Pennick, Edward Jerry. "The Struggle for Control of America's Production Agriculture System and Its Impact on African American Farmers." *Race/Ethnicity: Multidisciplinary Global Contexts* 5, no. 1 (2011): 113–20.

Perlo, Victor. *The Negro in Southern Agriculture: The Plantation, Sharecropping, Farm Labor, Land Ownership, Mechanization, and Living Standards since World War II.* New York: International Publishers, 1953.

Pierre-Louis, Lydie. "Farmers and Land Loss: A Historical Perspective of the Systematic Loss of African American Farms from the Nineteenth Century to the Present." *Encyclopedia of African American History* 2 (2009): 187–93.

Piven, Frances Fox, and Richard Cloward. *Poor People's Movements: Why They Succeed, How They Fail.* New York: Vintage, 1978.

Pohlmann, Marcus. *African American Political Thought.* Vol. 2, *Confrontation vs. Compromise: 1945 to the Present.* New York: Routledge Press, 2003.

Polletta, Francesca. "'Free Spaces' in Collective Action." *Theory and Society* 28, no. 1 (February 1999): 1–38.

Potori, Mary. "Feeding Revolution: The Black Panther Party and the Politics of Food." *Radical Teacher* 98 (2014): 43–50.

Price, Richard. *Maroon Societies: Rebel Slave Communities in the Americas.* 3rd ed. Baltimore: Johns Hopkins University Press, 1996.

Rabaka, Reiland. *Against Epistemic Apartheid: W. E. B. Du Bois and the Disciplinary Decadence of Sociology.* Lanham, Md.: Rowman & Littlefield, 2010.

Ransby, Barbara. *Ella Baker and the Black Freedom Movement: A Radical Democratic Vision.* Chapel Hill: University of North Carolina Press, 2003.

Rao, Hayagreeva, and Sunasir Dutta. "Free Spaces as Organizational Weapons of the Weak: Religious Festivals and Regimental Mutinies in the 1857 Bengal Native Army." *Administrative Science Quarterly* 57 (2001): 625–68.

Raper, Arthur Franklin. *Preface to Peasantry: A Tale of Two Black Belt Counties.* Chapel Hill: University of North Carolina Press, 1936.

———. *Tenants of the Almighty.* New York: Macmillan, 1943.

Reid, Debra A. "African Americans and Land Loss in Texas: Government Duplicity and Discrimination Based on Race and Class." *Agricultural History* 77, no. 2 (2003): 258–92.

———. *Reaping a Greater Harvest: African Americans, the Extension Service, and Rural Reform in Jim Crow Texas.* College Station: Texas A&M University Press, 2007.

Reid, Debra A., and Evan P. Bennett. *Beyond Forty Acres and a Mule: African American Landowning Families since Reconstruction.* Gainesville: University Press of Florida, 2012.

Reynolds, Bruce J. *Black Farmers in America, 1865–2000: The Pursuit of Independent Farming and the Role of Cooperatives.* RBS Research Report 194. Washington, D.C.: United States Department of Agriculture Rural Business–Cooperative Service, 2002. http://www.federation southerncoop.com/blkfarmhist.pdf.

Richardson, Clement. "Negro Farmers of Alabama: A Phase of Tuskegee's Extension Work." *Southern Workman* 56 (1917): 381–90.

Roll, Jarod. *Spirit of Rebellion: Labor and Religion in the New Cotton South.* Urbana: University of Illinois Press, 2010.

Rosengarten, Theodore. *All God's Dangers: The Life of Nate Shaw.* Chicago: University of Chicago Press, 2000.

Rosengarten, Theodore. "Our Promised Land." *Southern Exposure* 2 (Fall 1974): 22–32.

Ruffin, Kimberly. *Black on Earth: African American Ecoliterary Traditions.* Athens: University of Georgia Press, 2010.

Schwartz, Michael. *Radical Protest and Social Structure: The Southern Farmers' Alliance and Cotton Tenancy, 1880–1890.* Chicago: University of Chicago Press, 1988.

Scott, James C., and Benedict J. Tria Kerkvliet, eds. *Everyday Forms of Peasant Resistance in Southeast Asia.* London: Frank Cass, 1986.

Scott, Roy V. *The Reluctant Farmer: The Rise of Agricultural Extension to 1914.* Urbana: University of Illinois Press, 1970.

Sherrod, Shirley, and Catherine Whitney. *The Courage to Hope: How I Stood Up to the Politics of Fear*. New York: Atria Books, 2012.

Sitton, Thad, James H. Conrad, and Richard Orton. *Freedom Colonies: Independent Black Texans in the Time of Jim Crow*. Austin: University of Texas Press, 2005.

Slaughter, John. *New Battles over Dixie: The Campaign for a New South*. Lanham, Md.: Rowman & Littlefield, 1992.

Smith, Suzanne E. *Dancing in the Street: Motown and the Cultural Politics of Detroit*. Cambridge, Mass.: Harvard University Press, 2001.

Smock, Raymond. *Booker T. Washington: Black Leadership in the Age of Jim Crow*. Lanham, Md.: Rowman & Littlefield, 2009.

Sugrue, Thomas. *The Origins of the Urban Crisis: Race and Inequality in Postwar Detroit*. Princeton, N.J.: Princeton University Press, 1996.

Tapsell, Linda C., Elizabeth P. Neale, Ambika Satija, Frank B. Hu. "Food, Nutrients, and Dietary Patterns: Interconnections and Implication for Dietary Guidelines." *Advance in Nutrition* 7, no. 3 (May 1, 2016).

Tell, Long. *Black Song: Essays in Black American Literature and Culture*. Houston A. Baker, Jr., ed., Charlottesville: University Press of Virginia, 1972.

Thompson, Heather Ann. *Whose Detroit? Politics, Labor, and Race in a Modern American City*. Ithaca, N.Y.: Cornell University Press, 2004.

Tomich, Dale W. *Slavery in the Circuit of Sugar: Martinique and the World Economy, 1830-1848*. Baltimore: Johns Hopkins University Press, 1990.

Tullos, Allen M. "The Black Belt." *Southern Spaces*, April 19, 2004, http://www.southernspaces.org/2004/black-belt.

Vella, Christina. *George Washington Carver: A Life*. Baton Rouge: Louisiana State University Press, 2015.

Vincent, Stephen A. *Southern Seed, Northern Soil: African-American Farm Communities in the Midwest, 1765-1900*. Bloomington: Indiana University Press, 2000.

Vodicka, John. "The Federation of Southern Cooperatives Under Siege." *Southern Changes* 2, no. 8 (1980): 18-21.

Walker, Brian, and David Salt. *Resilience Thinking: Sustaining Ecosystems and People in a Changing World*. Washington, D.C.: Island Press, 2006.

Ward, Thomas J., and H. Jack Geiger. *Out in the Rural: A Mississippi Health Center and Its War on Poverty*. Oxford: Oxford University Press, 2016.

Washington, Booker T. "A Farmer's College on Wheels." *World's Work*, December 13, 1906, 8352-54.

———. "Industrial Education for the Negro." In *The Negro Problem*, 7-30. New York: J. Pott & Company, 1903.

———. "The Southern Letter XVI, no. 3 (February–March 1899)." In *Booker T. Washington Papers 1899–1900*, edited by Booker T. Washington and Louis Harlan, xxx–xx. Urbana: University of Illinois Press, 1976.

———. *A Town Owned by Negroes: Mound Bayou, Miss., an Example of Thrift and Self Government*. Baltimore: Johns Hopkins University Press, 1907.

———. "Twenty-Five Years of Tuskegee." *World's Work*, March 11, 1906, 7450.

———. *Up from Slavery: An Autobiography*. Garden City, N.Y.: Doubleday & Company, 1901.

———. "Winners from the Soil, Colored Heroes of the Farm—Benjamin Carr: He Crossed the Tobacco Bridge." *Negro Farmer*, July 7, 1914.

———. *Working with the Hands: Being a Sequel to "Up from Slavery," Covering the Author's Experience in Industrial Training at Tuskegee*. New York: Doubleday, Page & Co., 1904.

Westmacott, Richard. *African-American Gardens and Yards in the Rural South*. Knoxville: University of Tennessee Press, 1992.

White, Monica M. "D-Town Farm: African American Resistance to Food Insecurity and the Transformation of Detroit." *Environmental Practice* 13, no. 4 (2011): 406–17.

———. "Shouldering Responsibility for the Delivery of Human Rights: A Case Study of the D-Town Farmers of Detroit." *Race/Ethnicity: Multidisciplinary Global Contexts* 3, no. 2 (2010): 189–211.

———. "Sisters of the Soil: Urban Gardening as Resistance in Detroit." *Race/Ethnicity: Multidisciplinary Global Contexts* 5, no. 1 (2011): 13–28.

Wilkerson, Isabel. *The Warmth of Other Suns: The Epic Story of America's Great Migration*. New York: Random House, 2010.

Wood, Spencer D. "The Roots of Black Power: Land, Civil Society, and the State in the Mississippi Delta, 1935–1968." PhD diss., University of Wisconsin, 2006.

Woodruff, Nan Elizabeth. *American Congo: The African American Freedom Struggle in the Delta*. Chapel Hill: University of North Carolina Press, 2012.

Woodson, Carter G., and Rayford Whittingham Logan. "The Negro in Education." *Journal of Negro History* 5, no. 1 (1920): 1–21.

Woofter, Thomas Jackson. *Black Yeomanry: Life on St. Helena Island*. New York: Henry Holt and Company, 1930.

Index

Printed in the USA
CPSIA information can be obtained
at www.ICGtesting.com
CBHW061538010624
9427CB00005B/613